Praise for *Expectation Hangover*

"I wish I'd had this step-by-step guide on how to overcome huge obstacles when I shattered both my wrist and my dreams of playing for the NFL. Don't let your Expectation Hangover control your life — apply what is in this book!"

— Lewis Howes, former pro athlete turned lifestyle entrepreneur, host of *The School of Greatness* podcast

"Christine Hassler is the kind of true spiritual guide we all need in our corner — soulful, wise, compassionate, and practical. Her proven methods and deep personal understanding are like the best medicine ever for your heart and soul."

— Christine Arylo, self-love catalyst and author of *Madly in Love with ME: The Daring Adventure of Becoming Your Own Best Friend*

"Christine Hassler continues to be an invaluable voice for every generation. Her insights and observations have changed and enlightened the way I look at my life and the way I raise my children."

— Michael De Luca, film producer and Columbia Pictures president of production

"Disappointment can be a big, ugly monster hiding under our beds. This book is the go-to for getting us through Expectation Hangovers with grace and shining light to cast away those ugly creatures of disappointment!"

— Kathryn Budig, author of *The Women's Health Big Book of Yoga*

"Christine Hassler is brilliant and insightful. Finally, here is the solution for dealing with something that plagues so many, myself included. If you're hoping to thrive in a world that seems to hand out setbacks at every opportunity, this is the book for you. With transformational truths and real-life stories, *Expectation Hangover* will change the way you approach any challenge, giving you the courage and the wisdom to transform your life."

— Marcia Wieder, bestselling author of *Making Your Dreams Come True* and CEO/founder, Dream University

EXPECTATION HANGOVER®

ALSO BY CHRISTINE HASSLER

20 Something, 20 Everything
20 Something Manifesto

EXPECTATION HANGOVER®

Overcoming Disappointment in Work, Love, and Life

CHRISTINE HASSLER

Foreword by
LISSA RANKIN, MD

New World Library
Novato, California

New World Library
14 Pamaron Way
Novato, California 94949

Text design by Tona Pearce Myers

Library of Congress Cataloging-in-Publication Data
Hassler, Christine.
Expectation hangover : overcoming disappointment in work, love, and life / Christine Hassler ; foreword by Lissa Rankin, MD.
     pages   cm
Includes bibliographical references and index.
ISBN 978-1-60868-241-6 (hardback)
1. Disappointment. 2. Adjustment (Psychology) I. Title.
BF575.D57.H37 2014
152.4—dc23   2014018040

First printing, October 2014
ISBN 978-1-60868-241-6
Printed in Canada on 100% postconsumer-waste recycled paper

New World Library is proud to be a Gold Certified Environmentally Responsible Publisher. Publisher certification awarded by Green Press Initiative.
www.greenpressinitiative.org

10   9   8   7   6   5   4   3   2   1

CONTENTS

Foreword by Lissa Rankin, MD   xi

Introduction   xv
    What to Expect   xvii

PART ONE: EXPECTATIONS

Chapter One: My Expectation Hangovers   3

Chapter Two: The Whats and Whys of Expectation Hangovers   7
    "Expectation Hangover" Defined   8
    Why Expectation Hangovers Happen   11

Chapter Three: What Does Not Work   21
    Distraction   21
    Numbing the Pain   22

Being Strong   23

Pep Talks   23

The Next Best Thing   24

Spiritual Bypass   24

Chapter Four: Awareness and Acceptance   27

The First Step out of Disappointment   29

PART TWO: TREATMENT PLAN

Chapter Five: A Holistic Prescription for Treating
Your Expectation Hangover   35

Role-Playing Rx   39

Chapter Six: The Emotional Level   41

How We Suppress Emotions   45

Role-Playing Rx: The Surfer   49

But I'm Not Angry!   62

The Power of Vulnerability   64

Make a Date with Your Feelings   67

Conclusion   68

Chapter Seven: The Mental Level   69

Your Story   70

Role-Playing Rx: The Horseback Rider   74

Thought Time Travel   84

Conclusion   98

Chapter Eight: The Behavioral Level   101

Role-Playing Rx: The Scientist   103

Compensatory Strategies   117

Your Superpowers   126

Avoidance Traps   131

Your Core Values   133

Conclusion   140

Chapter Nine: The Spiritual Level   143
    The Goal Line versus the Soul Line   144
    Your Spiritual Curriculum   146
    Role-Playing Rx: The Seeker   149
    Living Inside Out   152
    Surrendering to a Higher Power   161
    Lesson Quest   168
    Your Life Purpose   171
    Conclusion   179

PART THREE: PREVENTION

Chapter Ten: Managing Your Expectations   183
    The Secret Sauce for Pursuing Goals   185

Chapter Eleven: Quick Fixes That Work   189
    Quick Fix 1: Stop People-Pleasing   189
    Quick Fix 2: Go Your Own Way   191
    Quick Fix 3: Don't Go to a Chinese Restaurant for Nachos 192
    Quick Fix 4: Wake Up from Comparison Comas   194
    Quick Fix 5: Be of Service   197
    Quick Fix 6: Be a Kid   198
    Quick Fix 7: Gorge on Gratitude   200

Conclusion   203

Acknowledgments   207
Notes   209
Index   211
About the Author   221

FOREWORD

I'm sure my loving parents meant well when they raised me to believe the world was my oyster. As the oldest child doted on by adoring parents, I grew up thinking the world would treat me as lovingly as my parents did, so imagine my surprise when I wound up in medical school, where I felt judged and criticized by my professors, who were regularly scolding me for my stupidity and incompetence. I also figured all men would treat me like the princess my father had led me to believe I was, so imagine my confusion and hurt when I wound up in a marriage with a man who didn't dote on me like my parents did.

By the time I was thirty-three years old, I was very successful in my career as a doctor, but I was twice divorced, professionally disillusioned, and taking seven medications for a host of health conditions my doctors led me to believe were incurable. Saddled with a serious case of entitlement, I felt like the Universe had let me down. By the time I was thirty-six, I wound up with one dark night of the soul after another that culminated in a massive

Expectation Hangover when the compounding losses left me humbled, emotionally paralyzed, and on my knees.

I thought I might find relief by quitting my job as a physician, selling my oceanfront house, and moving to the country, where I planned to launch my new career as a writer by penning my first masterpiece. But things didn't go as I planned, and by forty-one, I found myself $200,000 in debt, with no agent, no publisher, and a third failing marriage. My life had strayed so far from the fairy-tale life I had expected that I barely recognized it. Where had I gone wrong? My self-esteem took a major hit, and the shell of my ego started to crack. What I hadn't anticipated was that underneath that shell, the real gold had been buried all along.

I had to mine the gold from my Expectation Hangover one teensy nugget at a time before my life started to turn around. The process was slow, painful, and filled with self-judgment, disillusionment, frustration, roadblocks, and tests of my faith. Because my journey eventually yielded a great deal of personal, spiritual, and professional satisfaction, I can't regret a second of it, but I can say that I wish I had been blessed with Christine Hassler's book back when all this was happening. It might have saved me years of unnecessary suffering!

If this book has landed in your lap right now, and you're wallowing in an Expectation Hangover of your own, consider this a sign from the Universe that you're ready to press "fast-forward" on this phase of your journey. With this book, you will be guided through your Expectation Hangover with love, compassion, and sensitivity to how much you might be hurting right now. Nobody is going to expect you (or allow you) to skip your painful emotions with a "spiritual bypass." But by the time you reach the end of this book, you will have been given all the tools you need to mine the gold from your disappointment, as long as you're ready to face the honest truth about yourself and about what your soul may be here on this earth to learn.

After gleaning the gems from your Expectation Hangover, you'll not only heal from your disappointment but learn how to prevent future disappointment. You'll be inspired to live your life in a whole new way, and you'll become much more open to whatever smorgasbord of life experiences the Universe dishes up, rather than getting upset when you don't immediately get what you ordered off life's menu.

This book is your road map to navigate any disappointment you may be experiencing. I promise you that you are being called to participate in this adventure, and your mission, should you choose to accept it, will be more wondrous, magical, and filled with awe, mystery, purpose, and fulfillment than anything you could have dreamed up yourself. So take a deep breath, strap on your seatbelt, muster up your moxie, and get ready to let your Expectation Hangover take you on the ride of your life.

Everyone on a hero's journey needs a mentor, and Christine is the perfect guide as you walk your own path. As you practice the tools and exercises in this book, you will discover that you already have the love, fulfillment, and meaning that your soul intends to experience in this life. And you will have your Expectation Hangover to thank for how resilient, empowered, and courageous you have become.

I now look back at my Expectation Hangover with oodles of gratitude, and I know you will see yours in the same way when you've made it to life on the other side of disappointment, full of surprises and blessings you never could have expected.

— Lissa Rankin, MD, *New York Times* bestselling author of
Mind Over Medicine and *The Fear Cure*

INTRODUCTION

Have you ever had something turn out far different than you expected it would and felt immensely disappointed? Have you ever been so let down by a person or situation that you thought you'd never get over it? Have you ever not lived up to your own standards and felt a sense of failure?

Let's face it — life is full of surprises that are not always the kind we would wish for: A job and the financial security that came with it are gone. A relationship with the one we thought was "the one" suddenly ends or becomes the one thing we can't get right. A career path that was executed with precision becomes lackluster and tainted with doubt. A pregnancy that is wished for isn't happening. A project we poured our blood, sweat, and tears into doesn't bring the results we expected. A parent suddenly isn't there anymore, or a child doesn't live up to the potential we saw in him. An illness interrupts our life. Or we've checked off everything on our life checklist and still don't feel fulfilled.

We suffer when our reality does not match the expectations we are so attached to. If you can relate to this brand of discomfort — the kind fueled by a life drunk with expectations and the resulting crash we experience when things do not go as we planned or hoped — then you have experienced an Expectation Hangover®.

And you are not alone. I spent most of my life working hard to achieve personal and professional goals that I believed would make me feel happy and successful. My life unfolded according to the plan I worked hard to achieve. I did everything "right." However, when my career, engagement, finances, relationship with my family, and health came crashing down around me, I found myself in the midst of an Expectation Hangover I feared I would never overcome. And that was just my twenties!

"Since most of my friends are farther along in accomplishing their life goals than me, I feel behind in life, not as worthy as those who are fulfilling their goals. My self-confidence and trust in my own abilities have plummeted. I feel less motivated, energized, or excited to really work on figuring out what my path is. I feel confused, disconnected, and simply lost in regard to what I'm supposed to be doing."

— Athena

If you are anything like me, you have taken great comfort in planning and attempting to control life. We all take great pride in setting goals and achieving them. We find value in living up to the expectations of others, and security in others' living up to our expectations of them. But in those moments when things don't go as expected, not only do we feel disappointed, but we begin to doubt everything — including ourselves.

We internalize the lack of desired external results by making it mean we did something wrong or were wronged. This creates suffering that can range from tolerable to unbearable. Disappointment is indeed part of the human experience, but is the suffering necessary? It's easy to feel good when things are going well, but how do we reduce our suffering when they aren't? Is it possible to transform disappointment?

The answer is yes — *if* we learn how to leverage disappointment so we get something out of it rather than only suffering through it. Your disappointment might be the best thing that ever happened to you. Expectation Hangovers are doorways to tremendous opportunities to heal issues from our past, change how we are living in the present, and create a future based on who we truly are rather than who we expected to be. The problem is that we become so blinded by what we think we want, and paralyzed by the pain of not getting it, that we do not see the transformational door that is opening.

We pray for things to be different even though we stay the same. We exhaust ourselves by working hard to change our external circumstances without changing ourselves. The fear of encountering another Expectation Hangover can be paralyzing, so we remain in the discomfort of our suffering. But not facing our disappointment and apprehension about taking a step forward is far more damaging than anything we are afraid of. Ultimate fulfillment is only possible when we change the habituated thoughts and responses that keep us at a very base, survival level. You want to thrive, not just survive, don't you?

> "Some changes look negative on the surface, but you will soon realize that space is being created in your life for something new to emerge."
> — Eckhart Tolle

WHAT TO EXPECT

There are many inspirational stories about people who have overcome huge obstacles and are now living "happily ever after." We often hear the "before" and "after" story, but how did they get to the happy part? What exactly is the recipe for turning lemons into lemonade?

It begins with asking "What am I learning?" rather than "Why is this happening?" This question opens your mind to possibility and gets you out of feeling like a victim of your life. You can then *leverage* your disappointment rather than just attempting to get rid of it or wallowing in your suffering. This book is a step-by-step guide on how to do just that, on the emotional, mental, behavioral, and spiritual levels. Not addressing all these levels is like putting a Band-Aid on the Expectation Hangover, which increases the likelihood of reopening wounds from a particular disappointment at a later date.

Since we are not one-dimensional beings, I will be offering you a multidimensional approach that includes a range of tools and techniques. Make sure you have a journal to complete the written exercises in this book. I recommend handwriting your responses, rather than typing, as writing by hand helps you access the intuitive side of your brain. The book also includes guided visualizations that you can either read or download and listen to for free at www.expectationhangover.com/bonus. You'll learn to leverage your vast human potential by tapping into your logical, conscious mind, your intuition and creativity, and your loving, wise heart.

You have an innocent and playful side that is willing to be curious and try new things the way a young child does. You have a sensitive side that has taken things personally and deserves compassion. You have a warrior side that is courageously committed to positive change. You have a wise woman or man within you who has amazing insight and experience, and gently nudges you along, the way a loving parent would. And you have a spiritual side that can see everything from a place of detachment and acceptance.

I ask you to be willing to take this journey with me and to go at your own pace. I'm going to ask you to let go of your expectations. "But," you may say, "my expectations motivate me and help me achieve my goals." Not true. Let's make a distinction: An *expectation* is defined as "an eager anticipation for something to happen." A *goal* is defined as "a purpose or objective." When we are clinging to expectations, we are waiting for something to happen and giving our power away. As we start to identify and release our expectations, we can take more empowering steps toward achieving our goals, with a clear sense of purpose.

The Expectation Hangovers I have witnessed have deeply touched my heart and inspired tremendous compassion for the pain that is part of human experience. I am moved by what I have seen people face. You'll read many stories throughout the book about clients and their Expectation Hangovers. I too have experienced Expectation Hangovers and seen the blessings that come with them. But don't worry — I'm not just going to tell you that everything happens for a reason without showing you how to discover the reason. I'm here to teach you how to change the way you experience Expectation Hangovers so you can change your life. I'm here to inspire you with my story and the stories of others so you can actually get excited about the opportunities your Expectation Hangovers have in store for you. I'm here to relieve you of the expectations you are holding of yourself and others. I'm here to show you that the fulfillment you are seeking outside is much closer than you think. And most of all, I'm here to gently guide you out of suffering and into transforming your disappointment.

I cannot promise that after you finish this book, you will never have another Expectation Hangover, but I can assure you of two things. First, when you do experience disappointment, you will know how to move through it in a faster, more uplifting way. Second, the time between your Expectation Hangovers will increase. What you learn in this book will help you achieve a life that may not be free of disappointment but that will no longer be hindered by it.

Each of us has felt broken and bruised; and each of us has the inner resources we need to heal and transform. Every unfortunate circumstance can bring us great fortune. It is in the most undesirable of external circumstances that we discover internal qualities like courage, faith, compassion, inspiration, acceptance, and love. Life often throws us a curveball to get us to look in a different direction, one that is even better than we planned. Before that new direction is revealed, there is a window of opportunity — a chance to change behaviors that keep us in limiting patterns where we seem to face one Expectation Hangover after another. This is your window of opportunity.

"I've learned I was afraid of failure before my Expectation Hangover. I still am afraid sometimes, but I continue to make choices and try things because I am not paralyzed by my fear of failure anymore — it's happened, and I dealt with it. If it happens again, I'll deal with it again. The biggest blessing from my biggest disappointment is that I now have self-confidence and faith that I can handle anything. Until you see yourself go through something, you're never quite sure you can — now I am."

— Matthew

"To be alive is to be disappointed. You tried and failed and kept on trying, never knowing whether you'd ever get what you wanted. But sometimes we get what we need."
— Joan D. Vinge

Part One

EXPECTATIONS

Chapter One

MY EXPECTATION HANGOVERS

"I like living. I have sometimes been wildly, despairingly, acutely miserable, racked with sorrow, but through it all I still know quite certainly that just to be alive is a grand thing."
— Agatha Christie

I am no stranger to Expectation Hangovers.

Before the ink was dry on my college diploma, I moved to Los Angeles to pursue my dream of working in the entertainment industry. I was driven by a tremendous expectation of myself to be wildly successful to compensate for the insecurity I had been plagued with since childhood. By the ripe old age of twenty-five, I had an office with a view, an assistant who answered my phone, an expense account, a real salary, power lunches, television industry screenings, clients, and business cards. I dated and attended industry events. I even spent New Year's Eve with George Clooney — now there is a midnight kiss I will never forget! From the outside, it looked like I "had it all." There was just one problem: I was absolutely miserable.

Where were the happiness and worthiness I thought all my goals would deliver? Every day, I tried to talk myself into liking my job. I felt obligated to stay because I had worked so hard to get there, but I dreaded each day.

I started getting migraines, rode up the elevator to work with knots in my stomach, and was irritable all the time. To save myself from a total meltdown, and others from the bitch I all of a sudden was becoming, I quit.

Leaving my prestigious career changed my external circumstances, but I still found myself miserable. Burned out and craving a total change of direction, I became a personal trainer — I thought it might be my "passion." Wrong again. I then had nine different jobs in two years, constantly searching for something that would make me feel better about myself. During that time, I went into thousands of dollars of debt; got diagnosed with an "unknown autoimmune disorder"; stopped speaking to my mother after I made a decision that did not fit her expectations of me; and got dumped by my fiancé six months before our wedding. So there I was, now at twenty-seven: heartbroken, in debt, sick, at odds with my family, and lacking direction in my career. Nothing had turned out the way I expected, despite my meticulous planning and overachieving. Major Expectation Hangover.

One pivotal night I found myself, for the first time ever, contemplating how I could end my life. That was a terrifying thought, but I felt so incredibly hopeless and lost I did not know what to do.

And then something happened.

Suddenly and seemingly out of nowhere, a wave of unconditional love and compassion flooded over me. Time stopped. My pain was replaced with comfort. I knew that everything was indeed happening for a reason. Unlike the past, when people used that cliché on me and I felt like punching them and screaming, "Well, I don't know what the freaking reason is, and this sucks!" this time I *knew* it to be true — even if I did not yet know the reason. The feeling of peace and connection only lasted an instant because my mind came in to try and figure it out; but the impact of that moment will last a lifetime. For the first time in my life, I felt like I experienced God — and I had my Expectation Hangover to thank for it.

At that point, I made myself a promise to dig in, look at my life, and figure out who I really was, what I really wanted, and how I was going to get it. I opened my mind to the possibility that somewhere in the midst of this Expectation Hangover there could be a blessing. The first blessing revealed itself two days later when I woke up with the idea for my first book, which launched my very unexpected career as an author, professional speaker, facilitator, life coach, and spiritual counselor. My biggest Expectation Hangover was the catalyst for stepping onto a career path that I absolutely love.

My quarter-life crisis was behind me, and I believed I was on my way to creating the life I wanted. I broke free of debt, healed my relationship with my mom, and regained my health. After years of searching, I found my true passion in terms of work. And after recovering from a broken heart, I married a man I loved deeply. My thirties were looking the way I thought they should. I finally "had it all." (Ha! How cute of my ego to think that.) Then another Expectation Hangover began to emerge. Everything I expected to make me happy had manifested, yet I still felt a deep sense of longing for something I couldn't define. It was a thirst that could not be quenched by a job or a man or a paycheck or a trip to Bali (I've taken three). This Expectation Hangover had a deeper message for me. I embarked on a journey of learning how to leverage disappointment — a journey that shook me to my core.

The most notable fallout of this shake-up was a divorce that catapulted me further into the Expectation Hangover, which became the most severe I had ever experienced. I agonized over whether to get divorced so much that I lost half the hair on my head. But in my heart I knew our marriage had an expiration date (you'll learn more about those later in the book).

When I was going through my divorce, someone said to me, "Christine, milk this time for all it's worth." That was one of the best pieces of advice I received. The thing about an Expectation Hangover is that it is never just about the issue we are currently feeling hungover about — it triggers all kinds of juicy stuff from our past that has not yet been resolved.

This thirty-something Expectation Hangover included the perceived failure of a marriage, financial insecurity, and having no children despite hearing the loud ticktock of my biological clock. But I milked it for all it was worth. While grieving the demise of my marriage, I dived back into work at an accelerated speed, sold the home I had renovated with my husband, and moved into a place of my own — all the while showing up for people as a coach and inspirational speaker, which was not easy in the midst of my own Expectation Hangover. I was dealing with the shame I had about my "failed" marriage and had to quiet the "Who am I to give advice when my own life is not turning out the way I planned?" judgments. What I realized is that I am one of the best people to be teaching about Expectation Hangovers because I learned how to move *through* each one and walk through those doorways of transformation that were opening all around me.

When I wrote previous books, I felt I had proven techniques for overcoming Expectation Hangovers because I had created certain external results. But my most recent Expectation Hangover was different. This time I don't have a "happy ending" that would "prove" I treated my hangover effectively. But I am happier than I've ever been before because I've freed myself from suffering even though my life doesn't look the way I expected it would.

Even the things that feel absolutely miserable are in service to our growth, learning, and healing. The cure to Expectation Hangovers is *not* to figure out another way to get what we thought we wanted, but rather to move out of our own way enough to see what we really need.

> "Not until we are lost do we begin to understand ourselves."
> — Henry David Thoreau

Chapter Two

THE WHATS AND WHYS OF EXPECTATION HANGOVERS

"Sometimes things have to go wrong in order to go right."
— Sherrilyn Kenyon

We are all consumers of expectations. They are easy to come by — from parents, family, friends, the media — and many are self-created. Maybe it's to be successful, get married, have children, look good, make a difference, please others… The list is endless, especially in today's world, where there are constant opportunities to compare ourselves to others and look for ways to be more, better, or different. Never before have expectations been so high in terms of what humans are capable of, and this creates a paradox of opportunity and pressure.

Expectations are pervasive in our lives, and most of us are conditioned to be driven by them and to attempt to realize them. But we didn't start out that way. We are all born in a state of pure Love where there are absolutely no expectations. Think of it as our "original innocence." When you were born, you knew these Truths: You are whole and complete. There is absolutely nothing wrong with you. You are worthy and deserving. You can trust the Universe. You have a deep inner knowing. You are connected. All there is and all that matters is Love. You are Love.

And then you got older. And things happened that moved you out of love and into fear: someone criticized you; you only got praised for your accomplishments; someone left or wasn't there for you; you saw people fighting or got yelled at; your heart got broken; you were told your dreams were impossible; you felt incredible pressure to succeed; you got rejected; you made a mistake and judged yourself a failure; you compared yourself to others and believed they were better in some way. Or perhaps you had a blissful childhood and grew up expecting the adult world to be the same way. The moment you got your first reality check in the form of a disappointment was the moment you moved into fear.

When in the grip of fear, we experience disconnection and a sense of emptiness. The voice of our ego and the voices of others become much louder than our inner voice and Spirit, and we feel alone and separate. To manage the disconnection, we start to be driven by what we expect will make us feel loved again. To fill the emptiness, we create expectations of what we believe will fulfill us. Our expectations then become our compass, which often navigates us right into an Expectation Hangover.

> "When one door closes, another door opens;
> but we so often look so long and so regretfully upon the closed door,
> that we do not see the ones which open for us."
> — Alexander Graham Bell

"EXPECTATION HANGOVER" DEFINED

You probably have a good sense of what an Expectation Hangover is by now, but here is my official definition: the myriad undesirable feelings, thoughts, and responses present when one or a combination of the following things occurs:

- Things don't turn out the way you thought, planned, or wanted them to.
- Things do turn out according to your plans and desires, but you don't feel the fulfillment you expected.
- You are unable to meet your personal and/or professional expectations.

- An undesired, unexpected event occurs that is in conflict with what you wanted or planned.

There are many different types of Expectation Hangover, but they usually fall into one of the following three categories:

Situational Expectation Hangovers. These occur when something does not turn out the way we wanted or we do not get the anticipated satisfaction from achieving a result. Michelle worked so hard to pursue a career in law, but it turned out to be nothing like she expected; she found herself dreading going to work each day. Jason spent over a decade at a company and was promised a hefty promotion but was laid off with no warning.

Interpersonal Expectation Hangovers. This kind of Expectation Hangover occurs when we are let down by someone else or unpleasantly surprised by the actions of another. Jeff got a call that his son, who had always been his pride and joy, was arrested for drug possession. Sarah went on what she thought was a fantastic date but never heard from the guy again.

Self-imposed Expectation Hangovers. These occur when we do not live up to the standards or goals we have set for ourselves. In other words, we are disappointed in ourselves and the results we've achieved or failed to achieve. Richard spent a year studying for the medical school entrance exam but did not score high enough to get into the school of his choice. Chelsea gave her first presentation at work and left feeling like she completely dropped the ball.

Although the cast of characters and specific circumstances of an Expectation Hangover vary, the symptoms are generally similar to those of a hangover from alcohol but far more miserable and lasting:

- lack of motivation
- depression
- anxiety
- regret
- physical discomfort
- confusion
- irritability

- self-judgment
- denial
- addictive behavior
- lethargy
- anger
- shame
- guilt
- poor work performance
- diminished creativity
- strained relationships
- faith crises
- social withdrawal
- wanting to stay in bed, turn off the lights, and pull the covers over your head

Our beliefs and self-talk fuel a lot of the symptoms we experience during an Expectation Hangover. When things don't go our way, it is natural to buy into debilitating thoughts like "I am not enough," "I did something wrong," "Everyone else is better than me," "I'll be alone forever," "I'll never be successful," "Things never work out for me," and so on. If something unexpected happens to disrupt the image of who we think we are, we squirm, complain, and attempt to control it because our sense of identity is threatened. Our self-esteem plummets, and we may begin to feel disconnected from a Higher Power, or even question its existence entirely. We get caught up in regretting the past or latching onto the idea of something in the future we think will make us feel better. We'll do anything to end our suffering — the problem is we just don't know what to do.

EXERCISE
Identifying Your Expectation Hangovers

Now it's your turn to identify the Expectation Hangovers that are currently causing you the most suffering, by answering the following questions in your journal. For each yes, briefly describe the related Expectation Hangover and label it as situational, interpersonal, or self-imposed. Then, on a scale of 1 to 5, rate the level of disappointment it has caused (1 being bearable, 5 being tremendously painful).

1. Is there something in your life that did not turn out the way you planned?
2. Is there an aspect of your life that you are not enjoying even though you thought you would?
3. Is there someone in your life who let you down?
4. Is there a relationship that has taken a direction that is upsetting to you?
5. Are you disappointed because of something you have done or not done?
6. Do you regret a choice you made or an action you took?
7. Did something happen that caught you off guard and has left you scrambling or disrupted?

Before you considered these questions, you may have been aware of at least one major Expectation Hangover you have or had. Now you may realize there are several Expectation Hangovers you've been carrying around. Don't worry — once you know how to treat one, you will be able to navigate all disappointment with greater grace. For now, identify the Expectation Hangover you are suffering from the most. It will

"Would it all be different if I had done things differently? Would I be different if I didn't place so much pressure on myself? I said I never had expectations, but this feeling of loss can only mean that I did, or do."

— Melanie

be one you rated high on the disappointment scale (or the one you rated highest if there's only one with the highest rating). That is the one to focus on first.

· · · ·

WHY EXPECTATION HANGOVERS HAPPEN

"If a man will begin with certainties, he shall end in doubts;
but if he will be content to begin with doubts, he shall end in certainties."
— Francis Bacon

One of the most challenging parts of an Expectation Hangover is feeling that we've failed, that we haven't met the standards or goals we've set for ourselves — especially if we've poured our hearts into the attempt.

I spent three months putting together an online conference that I was passionate about. I conducted over thirty interviews, wrote tons of marketing materials and emails, produced a video, and hired a team of people. I truly expected 15,000 people to sign up for the conference. A week before the conference, we only had 2,500. I was so let down and could not figure out why we were not getting the results we'd expected. As I beat myself up and went into regret, thinking of everything I could have done or should have done, my Expectation Hangover got worse.

"I had so many illusions about my dream of changing the world through music and meaningful lyrics, and suffered constantly from an Expectation Hangover about not being paid or recognized for it. I was so focused on the outcome that I lost sight of how much I enjoyed creating music."

— Leslie

Yet I truly did *love* putting this project together. I had fun doing the interviews, met interesting new people, was enthusiastic about the subject matter, and produced a body of work I was proud of. But when the outcome wasn't what I'd expected, all of that went out the window, and I had an instant Expectation Hangover. Suddenly, the entire experience became about the destination and not the journey. Because my ego became obsessed with the numbers, I forgot about the joy, enthusiasm, and creativity that had lit up my soul.

Not getting our desired outcome is one of the *seemingly* cruel ways the Universe teaches us the lesson that the journey of life is more important than the destination. We feel so alive in those moments when we are pouring our blood, sweat, and tears into something we believe in. We feel inspiration, enthusiasm, and passion. Those are all wonderful things to experience, and we *like* the feelings that accompany them. But as soon as we realize that the dream we had our heart set on did not come true, all the good feelings evaporate into an Expectation Hangover, and we find ourselves asking, "Why is this happening?"

Good question. During my own Expectation Hangovers, I have wanted to know exactly why it was happening, both so I could do something about it and so I could counteract my uncomfortable feelings of uncertainty. We think that if only we knew *why* something was happening, we could change it and not have to endure the Expectation Hangover.

The main reason disappointment happens is to teach us paradigm-shifting life lessons. An Expectation Hangover is a wild card that causes us to start looking within and, ultimately, to turn in a different direction. On the surface Expectation Hangovers might appear to create disharmony, but they actually have a harmonizing effect because the unexpected is what leads to innovation and novelty.

We don't voluntarily sign up for the lessons Expectation Hangovers teach, because they threaten the things our ego clings to: control, security, and external results. Warning: the lessons I'm about to share won't be very satisfying to your ego and won't necessarily give you the kind of answers you desire. For now, I invite you to open your mind to understanding these lessons, and when we get to our treatment plan in part 2, you'll learn some tools for working with them.

"The entire time I was growing up, I was told that if I got a job making lots of money, if I found the right man, and if I had the right family, I would be happy. That if I stuck to 'The Plan,' I would be happy. Well, imagine my surprise when, as I got closer and closer to achieving The Plan, I felt farther and farther from being happy. I had the moneymaking job, the doting husband, the well-behaved child, and yet where was it? Where was this happiness I had been promised? The sense of fulfillment, purpose, achievement, contentment, and happiness was not there! Why not?"

— Connie

"Replace fear of the unknown with curiosity."
— Danny Gokey

Lesson 1: Control Is an Illusion

We are great at putting time and energy into achieving the results we want. And the more effort we put in, the more we feel entitled to get the results. When our expectations are met, we feel a sense of security and accomplishment; we feel safe and on track. We expect that life will evolve according to our plan and that people will behave in a predictable way. We all love control because the unknown is downright scary. In fact, I think control has become the master addiction. But the truth is we really don't have complete control over our lives, and nothing illuminates that truth more brightly than an Expectation Hangover.

Now, you may be thinking, "Of course I have control over my life. Don't tell me everything is determined by fate or some Higher Power."

Believe me, I hear you. My ego really likes to fight for control too. But in reality, it's an illusion. For example, you have an idea of what you are going to do tomorrow, but there are a million unexpected things that could happen to alter your plans. Am I saying that everything is up to some Higher Power? No, all of us have free will and therefore have influence over the course of our life. However, we do not have total control over when, how, or if certain events will happen. What we do have is total control over *how we respond* to what happens. But we put far more effort into attempting to control our life and make things happen than we put into taking responsibility for how we react to Expectation Hangovers. All the effort in the world will not always guarantee the result we desire.

"What I have realized from my Expectation Hangover is that you never really 'make it.' There is not some magical, safe point in life where you are just 'there' and don't have to worry anymore. Life and living are constant. Change is constant."

— Liana

When you stop grasping for certainty, a deeper sense of trust emerges. And I don't just mean trust in the Universe or a Higher Power; I mean trust in *yourself* and your own capacity to respond to life in an optimal way. Besides, if you knew everything that was going to happen, you would miss out on life's pleasant surprises.

OLIVIA'S STORY

About a year ago, I got fired. I'd never been fired from a job in my life, and I couldn't believe it was actually happening. I had worked so hard for my company, and after all my contributions — to be fired?! I felt betrayed, scared, confused, embarrassed, and like something was fundamentally wrong with me. I was also recently divorced and was now going to be responsible for my two small boys all on my own, with no job and no benefits. Since I felt so out of control, I went into a crazed overdrive of obsessively sending out résumés while internally beating myself up for being an awful human being who got fired. I applied for every job I could, even if it didn't seem like something I wanted to do. I wouldn't hang out with friends because I told myself I shouldn't be having fun until I found a job. I constantly worried about money and how I would feel secure again.

Things felt so out of control I finally allowed myself to ask questions like "Do you really want to take another job that will just pay the bills and keep you in the nine-to-five game for another thirty years? Or do you want to take notice, choose to see this firing as a gift, and give your life a hard shift in the direction of your dreams?"

Once I asked these questions and quit attempting to make something happen based on fear, random opportunities to take steps toward the things I really wanted to do, like being a doula, started showing up. These were things I had never pursued because they didn't feel secure enough. When I started noticing those incredible signals pointing me in the direction of my dreams, I paid attention and finally made a decision to stop trying to control every aspect of my life. I have learned the power and strength that come from walking through the fire of disappointment, pain, and fear. I know it's better to embrace change than resist it. Don't get me wrong; I don't always do it right away. But at least when I'm in resistance, I know I'm bringing it upon myself — which means I can also change it.

Lesson 2: Your Comfort Zone Is a Trap

We all have a comfort zone that we have constructed based on what feels safe and manageable. In this comfort zone, we make certain choices and engage in specific behaviors that reinforce feelings of security. It feels familiar; we know all the ins and outs. Occasionally, we will take a step beyond it, but usually only if we have made a careful list of pros and cons and feel a degree of safety about our level of risk. But our comfort zone does not feel comfortable because it is healthy; it feels so cozy because it is familiar and reinforces the illusion of control.

We are constrained by self-concepts and structures built from expectations about who we are supposed to be and what we are supposed to do. We long to feel the highs of love, joy, inspiration, and passion, but we do not want to feel the depths of uncomfortable feelings such as sadness, anger, and shame. We dream big dreams and desire change in our lives but limit ourselves because we are not willing to step into the unknown. So we continue playing it safe, living life according to our plans, and engaging in familiar routines and behaviors. Disappointment itself can become a comfort zone. As much as you want to treat your Expectation Hangovers, you may be experiencing a degree of complacency about the status quo, having resigned yourself to feeling let down by life; but that is no way to live!

Many of my clients come to see me because they want to change things in their lives. As soon as I suggest something that will create the desired changes but requires them to step out of their comfort zone, they come up with a million reasons why they can't do it. They stay trapped in their comfort zone, their vitality and sense of purpose withering away because they are not actualizing their potential.

Imagine a plant that has outgrown the pot it was planted in. What would happen? It would never grow into the plant it was destined to become unless it was replanted. Your comfort zone is like a shell of restriction, not protection. That's why I get so excited when someone has an Expectation Hangover; I know it's the Universe's way of making someone uncomfortable enough to bust out of their comfort zone of limitation so they can grow into their full potential. The human experience is one of continuous evolution. Within each of us there is an evolutionary impulse to transform. We are not static beings; change is unavoidable. If we resist or fear change, an Expectation Hangover comes along to help us evolve. No matter what your circumstances, do not settle for complacency or "good enough." You deserve and are capable of so much more.

Lesson 3: It Ain't Out There

Perhaps you can relate to the pattern of when/then and if/then thinking: When I get that raise, then I'll feel financially secure. When I get married, then I'll feel worthy. When I get a little more experience, then I can start my business. If I had not been laid off, then I would not be depressed. If I lose five pounds, then I'll feel confident. If I had not made that mistake, then I'd feel proud of myself. The number of when/thens and if/thens our ego can buy into is infinite.

Many people "work on themselves" so they can get something external. It's wonderful to have dreams, but when the inner work we do is designed solely to get outer results, we continue to experience Expectation Hangovers.

We think our happiness comes from getting what we want, and we often pursue our expectations at the cost of our health, relationships, and most of all, the present moment. Our obsession with what we can do, be, or have leaves us constantly looking for some external result. Then, once we get the things we think we want, we experience an Expectation Hangover if they are not as fulfilling as we thought they would be. Or we experience a short-term boost but then start looking for the next thing to strive for. It's an endless cycle.

Recently, I was hired to speak to a group of CEOs about "achieving fulfillment." I thought it was quite funny that they used the word *achieve* in reference to fulfillment — we're so attached to external results that we even try to "achieve" fulfillment! I began my talk with this very driven group by telling them we were going to meditate and then talk about love. The look on their faces was priceless!

Fulfillment is not something we make happen. Trying to measure up to all our internal and external expectations leaves most of us living as human *doings* rather than human *beings*. It is only when we have the courage to let go of what we expect to happen that we begin to experience the kind of fulfillment that lasts. Each Expectation Hangover is an opportunity to let go of something external that we have clung to for worth, safety, or love, and to find — *inside* ourselves — the experience we are looking for.

Lesson 4: You Are Not Being Punished

During an Expectation Hangover, we have a tendency to think we have done something to deserve the disappointment. We buy into the common misunderstanding that bad things happen to us to test us, or even as payback for something we did wrong. Most of us, whether consciously or unconsciously, carry around a fear that the Universe (or God, Spirit, or Higher Power) is judging us in some way. So when things don't go our way, we believe the suffering we experience is penance. This could not be further from the truth.

The truth is that *every* circumstance or situation is for your Highest Good — even if it doesn't feel like it at the time. The Universe does not punish, test, or keep a list of good/bad and right/wrong behavior. You didn't do anything wrong. You have always been doing the best you could. Really. Even if you do not totally believe this yet, begin to consider it. Beating yourself up and continuing to believe that you are being tested or punished will only perpetuate your Expectation Hangover and potentially make it worse. What appear to be tests and trials in your life are actually priceless gifts and teachings.

Sometimes what is for our Highest Good is a little humility. Our egos can create some rather unrealistic expectations of others and life in general. This can often lead to a sense of entitlement that will ultimately become alienating. A good, old-fashioned Expectation Hangover is just the reality check we need to stop thinking the world revolves around us.

Having been at his company for a year, Dylan expected to be treated with more respect, have his ideas taken more seriously, and receive a raise. He was frustrated and about to resign, but then he got fired for having a "bad attitude." Dylan not only was shocked, but also felt wronged. "How could they do this to me?" he was asking. I worked with Dylan on taking responsibility for his part in the situation by looking at how his expectations affected the way others perceived him on the job. I challenged Dylan to question whether his expectations were realistic, given that this was his first job out of grad school and that he was the youngest one at the company. As he took a step back and viewed the situation without taking it personally, he was able to see that he was coming across as having a sense of entitlement. Because Dylan was so focused on what he wanted and thought he deserved, he missed opportunities to be a team player. Fortunately, he was willing to leverage his disappointment and approach his next job search with humility. Four months later he was hired at a start-up where he works in an extremely collaborative environment and loves being a team player. He goes to work focused on what he can contribute rather than being obsessed with what he expects for himself. Keeping his expectations in check prepared him to thrive in this new environment. Disappointment may knock us off our pedestal pretty quickly if our expectations have gotten a little too self-focused and out of touch with reality. This is truly a blessing because, ultimately, a pedestal is a very lonely place to be.

Sometimes our expectations are based in fantasy, and we encounter an Expectation Hangover that feels like punishment when in reality it is saving us from future suffering. My client Jennifer was devastated when she confessed her feelings to a man she thought she was in love with and he rejected her. After her honesty and vulnerability, she felt very humbled and embarrassed, yet she eventually realized she was more in love with the *idea* of him than with the actual person. Her fantasy-based expectations of what their life together would be like kept her from seeing he was a bit of a player who had no intention of being in the kind of partnership she wanted. Although it was temporarily painful, she was eventually grateful to have the short-term pain instead of going into a relationship that most likely would have come with a lot of suffering.

Not clinging to fixed ideals helps you see more clearly because your vision is not obstructed by fear or desire. Jennifer decided she would be open to God putting the right person in her life instead of obsessively attempting to find him on her own. Ironically, just as she stopped searching for "the one," she found him. Two years after coming to me for help, she moved into a new apartment and married the man who lived across the hall.

Keep these lessons in mind and begin looking at your life as a grand adventure that offers many opportunities to grow. When we are committed to our values but set our expectations free, we create more space for unexpected opportunities that can lead to happiness rather than a hangover.

> "When you dance, your purpose is not to get to a certain place on the floor.
> It's to enjoy each step along the way."
> — Wayne Dyer

Chapter Three

WHAT DOES NOT WORK

"Numbing the pain for a while will make it worse when you finally feel it."
— J.K. Rowling

How do you treat Expectation Hangovers? Well, it takes a lot more than two aspirin, some greasy food, and staying inside with the lights low. There are ways to experience temporary relief from hangover-like symptoms, but for permanent relief a comprehensive treatment and prevention plan is required. This is quite different from the way most of us face our hangovers — struggling to endure them and looking for something or someone to make us feel better. So before we talk about what does work, we need to talk about what doesn't. The six most commonly used yet ineffective strategies for coping with Expectation Hangovers are summarized in this chapter.

DISTRACTION

An Expectation Hangover is the elephant in the room that you'd love to ignore. So instead of truly acknowledging it and facing it head-on, you channel all your energy into something else as a way to avoid it. You keep adding things to your to-do list, crowding out any contemplative space in your life.

"I gave up my job in Switzerland to be with my husband in the United States but found myself in the middle of a divorce just a year later. I kept myself very busy — too busy — so I wouldn't have to think about what went wrong. I worked full-time, studied part-time, and started to build my writing career. After almost two years of being a workaholic, I couldn't handle the stress anymore and crashed. I guess I still have some unfinished business to attend to, and I am doing it piece by piece now that I have some room to breathe and the strength to deal with it."

— Isabelle

Your life is full of busyness, not fulfillment. You take a vacation, hoping that a tan will rid you of your worries; you dodge conversations or connections with people that may require vulnerability; you find a project or person to obsess about, to remove the focus from your own pain; or you immerse yourself in some kind of adventure that will distract you from dealing with what is.

Consider: How do you distract yourself from focusing on your Expectation Hangover? How do you avoid truly dealing with disappointment?

NUMBING THE PAIN

Instead of diverting the pain of an Expectation Hangover, you may use some kind of numbing, or suppression, technique. Common methods of numbing include drinking, eating, working, spending money, watching TV, escaping with drugs (prescription or street), spending time on social media, internet surfing, and overexercising. Any kind of addictive behavior that keeps you from truly feeling is a form of suppression. Numbing is easy to do because there is no shortage of quick pick-me-ups and distractions. However, numbing is one of the most damaging coping strategies due to the high level of stimulation it involves. In order to maintain a particular level of suppression over time, you have to keep upping the ante and increasing the stimulation. So the longer you suppress by numbing, the more dependent you become on your suppression tool of choice.

"I was the 'other woman,' believing he would leave his girlfriend for me. When I realized this wasn't going to happen, I didn't want to get out of bed. Chocolate, wine, and TV became my best friends."

— Francesca

Consider: What substances or behaviors do you use to numb yourself? When you want to get rid of an unpleasant feeling or thought, what do you crave?

BEING STRONG

When something disappointing happens, we often buy into the assumption that we are being tested and that passing the test depends on pushing through and persevering, without giving ourselves permission to fully feel. We live in a world where being strong and pretending nothing is bothering us is not only common, but rewarded. "Be strong" is one of the most common pieces of advice I've heard, and it's one of my least favorite because the implication is we shouldn't feel. We put on a mask, trying to look strong on the outside while falling apart on the inside. Being strong is overrated. Pushing away an Expectation Hangover usually means you're going to be pushing aside some valuable learning and healing. Vulnerability is a powerful tool for healing. Harshness and mental toughness diminish vulnerability. Perseverance is important when leveraging Expectation Hangovers, but the key is to persevere *through* your Expectation Hangover rather than mustering the strength to push it away or jump over it.

"On the outside I acted like it was all fine — I was a tough girl. Everyone said, 'Oh, it will just take time.' I stopped sharing any feelings because I thought I just needed to be strong."
— Glenda

Consider: Have you been told by others, or do you tell yourself, to "be strong" when you have an Expectation Hangover? What are the costs of "being strong"? What does vulnerability mean to you?

PEP TALKS

We understand the power of positive thinking because our thoughts have energy. However, when we are in the eye of an Expectation Hangover storm, giving ourselves a pep talk is not always appropriate and can be a form of avoidance. I see many people put pressure on themselves to move immediately into reciting positive affirmations, but it does not feel authentic in the midst of disappointment. Don't get me wrong — I am not advocating negative thinking or indulging in a pity party. What I am saying is that acknowledging what is truly authentic for you is an important part of your healing. Pressuring yourself to think completely positive thoughts will most likely trigger self-judgment because it is an unrealistic expectation.

Consider: When experiencing an Expectation Hangover, are you quick to find a way to "make everything okay"? Does positive thinking feel sustainable and believable? If you could give yourself permission to acknowledge that you don't like what is happening, would that be a relief?

THE NEXT BEST THING

When we don't like what is happening, we often assume that we just need a new set of circumstances. A new job, a new city, a new relationship, a new car — "the next best thing." Even if you move to a new city, get a new job, start a new relationship, or invest in a big purchase, that external thing is only a replacement, not a solution, because you're still carrying around all the unresolved internal issues from your Expectation Hangover. Trying to replace the pain of one thing with the pleasure of something else will not create lasting positive results in your life.

"Instead of dealing with the hurt and betrayal from my breakup, I thought the best way to get over someone was to get under someone else. Yet each new relationship I created felt meaningless and disappointing, so I ended up still feeling miserable, and lonely too."

— Sophia

Why not? Because what motivated and attracted the new thing was your disappointment and feeling of lacking something. And that's like building a house on sand. It may stand for a while, but sooner or later, the house will sink because it isn't built on a strong foundation.

Consider: When have you attempted to treat an Expectation Hangover by seeking out "the next best thing"? How did it work out for you? Are you searching for something external to cure your disappointment?

SPIRITUAL BYPASS

When we have an Expectation Hangover, we sometimes take a "spiritual bypass," attempting to jump immediately to the blessings of the situation without doing the work that actually facilitates the kind of learning that creates lasting changes in our life. In my experience we cannot solely meditate, chant, or pray our way out of an Expectation Hangover. Spiritual practices are key, but we are multidimensional beings. If we attempt to see the silver lining too soon, we may be turning away from the truth of our human experience. Just as our Expectation Hangovers involve a range of experiences, we have to be willing to address them on a range of levels — emotional, mental, and behavioral, as well as spiritual.

Consider: Are you attempting to repress your negative thoughts, immediately looking for the blessing? Do you believe you should not feel bad — or even experience guilt for "indulging" in your feelings? Are you relying on some spiritual practice to cure your Expectation Hangover?

You have probably used at least a few of the above coping strategies at different times. And you're in good company. We all employ these strategies because we are never really taught how to deal with disappointment effectively. Because Expectation Hangovers don't feel good, we look for an expedient way to ease the discomfort. If you deny, judge, or resist your process and what an Expectation Hangover is catalyzing within you, you may actually amplify your symptoms. Left untreated, Expectation Hangovers continue to affect you and influence your thoughts, feelings, decisions, and reactions. Furthermore, you will continue to unconsciously re-create different versions of the same Expectation Hangover.

> "Character cannot be developed in ease and quiet.
> Only through experience of trial and suffering can the soul be strengthened,
> vision cleared, ambition inspired, and success achieved."
> — Helen Keller

Chapter Four

AWARENESS AND ACCEPTANCE

"Life is simple. Everything happens for you, not to you. Everything happens at exactly the right moment, neither too soon nor too late. You don't have to like it…it's just easier if you do."

— Byron Katie

Now that we've established that Expectation Hangovers hold keys for transformation, I know you'd love to jump right to the fulfillment part. But, trust me, if you want *lasting* fulfillment — the kind that is not based on any external outcome — allow yourself the time and dignity of your process. *You* are worth it.

Begin by becoming fully aware of what your Expectation Hangover is and how it is affecting you. *Awareness* means "having knowledge or cognizance." The more you understand your Expectation Hangovers, the easier it is to treat yourself and alleviate negative symptoms.

Just as a doctor would have you fill out an intake form and ask you a lot of questions about your medical history and current symptoms, you must comprehensively assess your Expectation Hangover in order to treat it effectively. Let's begin by examining how your Expectation Hangover is affecting you on the emotional, mental, behavioral, and spiritual levels.

✳ **EXERCISE**
Expectation Hangover Assessment Form

Refer back to the answers you wrote for the Identifying Your Expectation Hangovers exercise (p. 10) and, for each Expectation Hangover you identified, answer the following questions comprehensively.

1. What caused the Expectation Hangover? Name the Expectation Hangover (for example, "Not Getting the Job I Wanted") and write the name at the top of your assessment form.

2. What specifically were the expectations you had of yourself and/or of someone or something else?

3. What thing that happened or didn't happen is contributing *most* to your Expectation Hangover?

4. Of the six temporary coping strategies discussed in chapter 3, which ones have you been using?

5. What feelings are you experiencing?

6. Describe the current state and theme of your thoughts: Are they in the future or the past? Are they supportive or critical? Are they positive or negative? What are you obsessing about?

7. What do you believe about yourself as a result of your Expectation Hangover?

8. What do you believe about others and/or life in general as a result of your Expectation Hangover?

9. What conclusions have you drawn as a result of your Expectation Hangover (for example, "I shouldn't have trusted that person," "I don't get what I want," "Life isn't fair").

10. What actions are you taking or not taking as a result of your Expectation Hangover?

11. How has your Expectation Hangover impacted your faith or your connection to a Higher Power?

12. Does this Expectation Hangover remind you of things from your past? Are certain memories surfacing? How does this feel familiar?

13. How do you perceive your future now? When you think about what's ahead, what do you see?

This assessment form is your awareness tool. Keep it handy because you will refer to it as we move into the treatment plan.

• • • •

THE FIRST STEP OUT OF DISAPPOINTMENT

Have you ever practiced martial arts? One of the core principles is that instead of resisting a punch that is thrown at you, you should accept it and follow the energy of the punch because resistance takes more energy than acceptance. A punch hurts more if we resist it. Similarly, when you move into acceptance of your disappointment, there is no resistance of what is, so you have far more energy to treat your Expectation Hangover.

Acceptance does not mean you have to like the circumstances and symptoms of your Expectation Hangover; rather it means being free of judgment about it. What is judgment? Each time something happens and we form an opinion about it, or label it as "good," "bad," "right," or "wrong," we are judging and resisting what is. There is what happens (reality), and then there is the meaning we make of it (our interpretation of reality). Our judgments feel true to us, but they are really only beliefs we create. These limiting interpretations of reality keep our Expectation Hangover in a stagnant state, making it more difficult for us to transform.

From a very young age, we are taught about right and wrong, and rewarded for being "good." It feels natural to judge because our egos long for reassurance, and judging something gives us a false sense of certainty. Our desire for certainty can hinder our evolution because judgment locks in emotions, beliefs, and behaviors that cause and perpetuate disappointment. Judging — ourselves, others, and the world — is so pervasive it has become our default mode.

Think of your Expectation Hangover and consider your judgments about it: Do you think it shouldn't have happened? Do you think it was terrible? Do you believe things should have been different? Do you think you were wronged? Do you think you were wrong? Do you believe it caused undesirable circumstances in your life? Do you see yourself as damaged by it? If you answered yes to any of these questions, then judgment is perpetuating your hangover.

You may be thinking, "The thing that caused my Expectation Hangover

"Being my partner's caregiver after his brain injury has been far more traumatic than my military experience. I have so much trouble accepting he is not dead but no longer the man I knew, accepting there would be no recovering our dreams. I need to make a brand-new plan to include the new set of circumstances. I can only accept all things. Blaming myself is not the answer. Accepting my own true nature as love opens my heart to give love and receive love. I realize I am the cause of my own suffering. When I compartmentalize the pain and take ownership as opposed to blame, I open myself up to a perspective that allows me to move forward instead of stagnating."

— Didi

was awful — I can't imagine accepting it!" What is key to understand is that acceptance does not mean you condone or agree with what happened. Rather, acceptance means you stop trying to make meaning out of what happened or didn't happen, and you put aside the opinion that things should or shouldn't have gone a certain way. Acceptance means letting go of judgment and your attachment to labeling things "good," "bad," "right," or "wrong." Acceptance means you choose to no longer employ temporary coping strategies to fight your Expectation Hangover.

Moving through this book and treating your Expectation Hangover effectively will be much easier if you hold an unconditionally accepting, open-minded, and expansive attitude toward yourself, others, and reality as a whole. Things have been hard enough so far, haven't they? Choose the grace plan: move into acceptance.

※ **EXERCISE**
Moving into Acceptance

This exercise will help you move into acceptance so you can complete the treatment plan in part 2 effectively.

1. What are you judging about your Expectation Hangover? In other words, what do you think should or shouldn't have happened? List all of your opinions and judgments about the situation in your journal.

2. Think of a time when things didn't exactly go your way but you accepted it rather than fighting it or going for a quick fix. It can be something as big as not fighting for a promotion you didn't get or

something as seemingly small as not getting upset over a flight being late. Bring to mind a time when you simply accepted what was. Then close your eyes and really enliven the memory by visualizing it in great detail until you are experiencing what acceptance feels like.

3. Once you are in the feeling of acceptance, look over the list you wrote in response to the questions in step 1 and rewrite it, using the phrase "I am willing to accept" before each statement. For example, "I am willing to accept that I was dumped," "I am willing to accept that I didn't get a promotion," "I am willing to accept that I wish I made a different choice." *Remember*: acceptance does not mean you have to like it; it just means you are releasing resistance against what is.

4. Acknowledge yourself for being willing to change your point of view from one of judgment to one of acceptance. Notice what a relief it is to stop resisting and judging.

• • • •

DENISE'S STORY

You could say I've been kind of a control freak from day one. Growing up, I was always "the boss." In fact, my brother had a special acronym for me that clearly affirms my natural tendencies: SCMCOTU (Supreme Commander, Master Controller of the Universe). I shudder to imagine the challenge I was for my parents.

I learned the ultimate lesson of surrendering control and leaning into acceptance when I had an unexpected and traumatic cesarean birth. My plans for a natural birth in water, for immediate skin-to-skin contact with my baby, for inviting my child into a world of peace, tenderness, and love were shattered. Our baby girl was born into the hands of a stranger, shielded from me with a curtain, and cut out of my womb by a doctor I had never met. Never did I expect for my baby girl to join us under such conditions. Never did I expect to feel so completely out of control. Never did I expect to feel like such a failure and such a success at the same time.

Once I began to face my sadness, my feelings of utter failure, and my desperate desire to have had the birth I planned, I could see that I was completely ignoring the most important truth: though my child's birth did not follow the plans I'd held on to so desperately, everything turned out wonderfully, and I have a beautiful, healthy baby girl. What better way for me to learn to release my expectations than to see my plans shattered? How could I truly embrace the art of surrender without being taught so clearly that grace comes from letting go?

You have a powerful choice to make right now: either accept your Expectation Hangovers fully or fight against them. My sense is you are exhausted from fighting, but perhaps you think you have to stay strong. I assure you that surrendering through acceptance is one of the most powerful things you can do. Your life doesn't have to be a battle. You don't have to work so hard or be so hard on yourself. If you feel stuck in situations that keep repeating themselves, it is a sign of a core issue that holds deep truths and life lessons for you. When you attempt to eliminate your suffering by fighting with reality, you lose 100 percent of the time.

> "We must accept finite disappointment but never lose infinite hope."
> — Martin Luther King Jr.

Part Two

TREATMENT PLAN

Chapter Five

A HOLISTIC PRESCRIPTION FOR TREATING YOUR EXPECTATION HANGOVER

"If we will be quiet and ready enough, we shall find compensation in every disappointment."
— Henry David Thoreau

Even before your Expectation Hangover hit, you might have been creating external results and achieving success in certain areas, but still not feeling a sense of fulfillment. Nothing felt terribly wrong, yet nothing felt particularly right either. Then, once an Expectation Hangover hit, you felt out of balance and like a lot was missing. To me balance is about harmony between our emotions, thoughts, actions, and soul. We feel out of balance whenever there is an excess or deficiency in any of those areas.

The treatment plan offered in this book is a holistic approach to creating harmony even in the midst of the chaos of an Expectation Hangover. It's not enough to engage in thoughts or actions to try to fix the symptoms; you also have to address the emotional components of an Expectation Hangover. Similarly, it is not effective to focus on our emotions and not engage in any behavioral changes or seek deeper understanding. Most of us learn and adopt highly ineffective ways to deal with our emotions, manage our thoughts, take action, and connect with a Higher Power. When it comes to our negative emotions, we develop ways to avoid and suppress them. When it comes to our thoughts, we allow our mind to control us, tell us things that are not true, and make us worry, obsess, and overanalyze. When it comes to our behavior, we operate out of habits based on stories we believe about ourselves and the way the world works. And when it comes to our spiritual life, we may be uncertain about faith, focusing more on our physical reality and only reaching out to God when we need something.

This treatment plan will help you leverage your Expectation Hangover, not just get over it. You will learn how to express and release your emotions in a healthy way. You will begin practicing mindfulness by knowing that you have dominion over your thoughts. You will begin creating different results in your life by shifting your actions and changing what drives your behavior. You will identify or deepen your connection to a Higher Power and begin to understand your life from a spiritual perspective — which is liberating!

You have emotions, but you are not your emotions. You have thoughts, but you are not your thoughts. You have a body, but you are not your body. You have relationships, a career, and belongings, but you are not your relationships, your career, or your belongings. You are a spiritual being having a human experience. Even if you do not believe in God, you are aware that there is a bigger picture in life. You have felt it at times in nature, when your child was born, when a prayer was answered, or when you've truly felt love for another. If you feel resistance at any time to the truths and tools I share, ask yourself if the way you are reacting to your Expectation Hangovers is working for you. Do you feel peaceful? Fulfilled? Accepting? Connected? Loving? Loved? Purposeful? If the answer is no, it's time to stop letting resistance run the show.

HILARY'S STORY

I was a checklist kind of girl, with my life mapped out before me. I was a people pleaser and wasn't listening to my intuition. My hangover hit when a relationship ended unexpectedly. Everything began to unravel after that, as I had put so much of myself into an idea, a projection of a thought, that

I didn't know how to hold myself up while the walls of my expectations were falling around me. Little did I know this experience was the beginning of my awakening to myself. I made what felt like an impulsive but intuitive decision to move to New Zealand and try to make a go of my teaching degree. I had no job, no home, and no one to go with me; I just knew that this was what I had to do. My year there was the most transformational experience I have ever had.

Letting intuition and faith guide me, I found a home, a family, and a job at a Montessori school (until then I wasn't even aware that alternative schools existed). I reconnected to my love of teaching and truly got to understand what education can be and what kids deserve out of learning and guidance. Traveling and immersing myself in an entirely new environment, with new people, allowed me to get out of my head and enabled me to begin feeling again. I started to eat healthier and ran to the ocean almost every day. I talked to Spirit and my intuition, expressing my feelings and asking for guidance. By the end of my year abroad, I felt completely healed.

My time in New Zealand opened me up to a world where anything is possible, where life is not a matter of checking off a list, but a journey of continuously learning, challenging myself, and accepting the forks in the road as gifts of fulfillment. I know now that happiness comes from within and that it is expectation-less. The word expectation *will have little relevance in my life. Intuition and love are the things I build my life with now.*

You are your own greatest ally in navigating through your Expectation Hangovers. No one knows what is best for you other than you. You have forgotten that, because you've been so busy trying to live up to all the expectations you feel. You cannot hear the voice of your intuition because your expectation-driven thoughts are too loud. You have been looking outside yourself for answers. They are not out there. It is by going within that you find out who you really are. It cannot be discovered in a job, a relationship, or any other external thing. Part of the way your Expectation Hangover serves you is by removing something external to reorient you back to your own internal compass, which will always lead you in the best direction.

GUIDED VISUALIZATION
Connecting to Your Internal Compass

You can download the audio version of this exercise at
www.expectationhangover.com/bonus

You've been conditioned to look outside yourself for direction. Now it's time to reorient. This visualization exercise will help you connect to your internal compass — the part of you that always offers you the best guidance. Read all the directions so you understand them, then take yourself through the exercise.

1. Find a quiet, comfortable place to sit where you won't be interrupted.

2. Close your eyes and take five deep, slow breaths. Bring yourself into the present moment by focusing your awareness on your breath. Feel each inhalation and exhalation.

3. After you feel more calm and present, visualize some kind of volume control device located in your mind that goes from 1 to 10. Maybe it's a dial, a lever, a knob, or a touch pad. Whatever you see is perfect. This volume control represents the level of noise of your thoughts. What number is it at now? If your thoughts are loud, it's probably at 9 or 10. Wherever it is, is perfect.

4. Next, in your mind's eye, visualize yourself turning down the volume of your thoughts. See the dial, lever, knob, or touch pad decreasing the volume of your thoughts, 10, 9, 8. Keep focusing on your breathing, seeing each number as you go down, 7, 6. Soften your belly even more, 5, 4. Your thoughts are getting quieter. Increase the volume of your breath as you decrease the volume of your thoughts, 3, 2, 1, 0. Feel the stillness of your mind. Experience the quietness of presence. Hear the sound of your soothing breath.

5. Bring one hand to your abdomen, just a few inches above your navel. Breathe into that part of your body. This is your internal compass. Your internal compass will offer you directions that will come in the form of a sensation, a feeling, an image, or even a word or

phrase you may hear inside. At first you may not feel anything; but as you practice this exercise and establish this connection, you will. For now just spend some time experiencing how it feels to be a little more out of your head.

6. Your connection to your internal compass is anchored by the hand you have resting on your abdomen. Take one more rich, deep breath into this place so you can feel your hand rise. Inwardly, say, "I always know what is best for me. I trust myself."

7. When you are ready, slowly open your eyes and bring your awareness back into the room.

8. Take some time to reflect on this process in your journal.

. . . .

"You're braver than you believe, and stronger than you seem,
and smarter than you think."
— A. A. Milne

ROLE-PLAYING Rx

Now that you are beginning to reorient yourself from the inside out rather than the outside in, you are ready to dive into your treatment plan. The most effective prescription tool I have developed to respond to Expectation Hangovers holistically is called "role-playing Rx." This method uses the metaphor of a familiar role — one whose basic activities, mind-set, and skills you're acquainted with — to help you understand how to do things that may be unfamiliar to you.

Most of us need a picture we can relate to, to help us transform our emotions, thoughts, behavior, and relationship with a Higher Power. Stepping into familiar roles with new viewpoints and strategies is an effective way to gain altitude on situations where we feel highly charged. Role-playing Rx will also allow you to think more creatively and use your right brain more, thereby giving your rational, analytical left brain a rest.

Throughout this treatment plan, I will also be sharing "transformational truths," which are principles that will reduce the severity and length of your Expectation Hangovers. These truths will help you perceive your disappointment in a way that assists you in moving through it faster. We all know that being "book smart" means being able to succeed scholastically, which creates external results. But being book smart only gets us so far, and, as a 4.0 student, I can attest that it definitely does not prevent disappointment. In order to be life smart, we must see beyond the illusions of our judgments and conditioning by keeping these transformational truths in mind.

We get so caught up in the disappointment of our Expectation Hangovers that possibilities pass us by. We waste time on mindless activities, like tweeting while stuck in traffic, gossiping, and making to-do lists that really aren't helping us do much. We stuff our schedule with fillers rather than spending time on things that are truly fulfilling. We rely on ineffective coping strategies. We complain about our outer circumstances because we forget we have the power to change our inner experience at any time.

The techniques in part 2 are all about actualizing your potential by committing to no longer settling for mediocrity or complacency. It is time to milk your Expectation Hangover for all it's worth rather than wallowing in it. As your coach, I am enthusiastically calling you forward and offering you new tools to deal with old emotions, thoughts, and patterns. It's actually quite easy to leverage your disappointment in a way that supports you in optimizing your potential, but it requires commitment on your part. Challenge yourself. Do things that push you out of your comfort zone — change *never* occurs within the walls of your comfort zone. Commit to learning new things. Develop skills that do not come naturally to you. Treating your Expectation Hangovers is not about changing your reality, but about changing your reaction and responses to it so that true transformation occurs.

Chapter Six

THE EMOTIONAL LEVEL

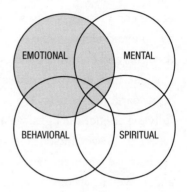

"The walls we build around us to keep sadness out also keep out the joy."
— Jim Rohn

An Expectation Hangover catalyzes and magnifies feelings that most of us would identify as undesirable. (From my perspective, there are no "positive" or "negative" emotions, but for the sake of clarity I will use those words in this chapter to describe the feelings we desire more and the feelings we desire less, respectively.) Since no one enjoys feeling bad, the immediate impulse is to get out of the negative feeling as soon as possible instead of fully experiencing it. This is because we do not know how to manage our feelings in a way that leads to healing through expression, understanding, compassion, and forgiveness. Plus, we often consider strong emotions to be dangerous territory — we're afraid they'll move us closer to being crazy, hysterical, or losing control.

We try to put distance between ourselves and our emotions in all sorts of ways. We overthink or overanalyze our feelings, to stay in our minds. We deny the emotions we don't want to experience by pretending we are "FINE" (Feelings Inside Not Expressed). We throw ourselves pity parties and become victims. We numb ourselves with behaviors, sometimes to the extent that they become addictions. We criticize and judge ourselves, or blame or judge others. But avoiding feelings pushes them below the surface of our consciousness, where they continue to do damage. And the harder we try to avoid feelings, the deeper we push them. This can lead to unhealthy thoughts and behaviors, and even to illness.

The human experience is all about contrast: yin/yang, male/female, light/dark, joy/sorrow. Every dark emotion has a light side; and in order to fully experience the light, we must journey through the darkness. If we stop resisting, we can find unexpected insights and gifts in the darkness. We know joy because we understand sadness. We know peace because we understand anger. We know compassion because we understand shame. Remember, we are not one-dimensional beings — we are here to experience the full range of emotions.

PATRICIA'S STORY

After being laid off due to corporate downsizing, I decided to travel abroad to fulfill a lifelong dream of immersing myself in another culture while also escaping the uncertainty I felt from not having a job for the first time in twenty years. I had anticipated that traveling would be enlightening and exotically romantic. The reality was far lonelier and more disillusioning than I ever could have imagined. However, physically removing myself from the constant hustle and obligations of home was like an "out-of-life" experience — I had the opportunity to view my life from a fresh angle, to pause from the go-go-go and take stock.

Pausing was not something I was used to. Within thirty-six hours my world had become quiet — and I felt like a junkie going through detox. Long-suppressed emotions bubbled to the surface. The lid came off of feelings that had been ignored for decades. Some days I was overwhelmed by anger, sadness, hurt, and anxiety. My stomach would be in knots, and I would lose my appetite. The hardest part was dealing with the shock of how lonely and sad I felt after finally realizing my lifelong globe-trotting dreams. I did not antici-pate that all the internal issues I was trying to run away from would follow me halfway across the world. I had no choice but, for the first time in my life, to allow my feelings to breathe. I gave them space, I sat with them, and I honored them. I found the courage to be vulnerable. Often I was terrified of what I would feel, but my feelings were grateful for permission to express themselves.

Some days I would come home from a good run and just sit and cry. It was an incredible release. I discovered a lot of compassion for myself. I did a lot of writing. I set off on my adventure with the intention of writing a travel blog while I was overseas, but I mostly wrote about things I had struggled with back home. I actually had enough time to process everything and enough perspective to begin to make sense of it. I returned home with a six-hundred-page non-travel, feeling blog.

The biggest lesson from my Expectation Hangover was that the most effective route to the other side of pain is through it. I had put so much effort into avoiding yucky emotions — by numbing, suppressing, ignoring, and not having time for them — that I was also cutting myself off from feeling joyful, inspired, and alive. It is now crystal clear to me that no matter how extremely you change your external circumstances — even if you wake up every morning sipping Turkish tea as the sun rises over the Bosporus — ultimately, you need to embrace your own truth and love your sadness if you truly want to be happy. Knowing that happiness cannot be found outside of me has radically shifted my expectations and helped me realize the limitations of changing my external life. I am grateful that I had the courage to actually feel my pain because now, even as an unemployed, single, forty something, I am actually happier than I have ever been before.

Your emotions are incredibly valuable. They deserve your compassion, your attention, and your patience. They deserve to be expressed. By "expression" I do not mean talking on and on about your emotions. I'm sure you have analyzed yourself so much that by now you could write an autobiographical self-help book! It feels safer to *talk* about our emotions — why we are sad, who we are angry at, why we have a right to be angry — than to experience them. However, you leverage your Expectation Hangover on the emotional level by giving yourself full permission to experience your feelings in a safe and loving way.

There are two things to consider as you journey through the emotional treatment plan for your Expectation Hangover. First, don't compare your life experience to anyone else's. You may think it's silly to cry over being laid off when you know someone who just lost a child to cancer. It is not: your experience is your experience. Understandably, hearing about other people's struggles puts our lives in perspective and cultivates gratitude, but that happens in our left brain, our rational mind. Feelings come from your right brain, the emotional side. Minimizing your emotions in light of someone else's journey is a form of suppression. For now, honor your personal Expectation Hangover and give yourself full permission to feel all your feelings about it.

Second, expect that the symptoms triggered by your Expectation Hangover will be tied to feelings you stuffed away in your past. Expectation Hangovers catalyze feelings that you have been unwilling or unable to face before. Your treatment plan on the emotional level gives you the opportunity to work through them so there is more room for the feelings that feel good!

Working on the emotional level was a very important part of treating my own Expectation Hangovers. At eleven years old I was diagnosed with depression and put on Prozac. For twenty years I took a variety of antidepressants, which numbed feelings of sadness and anger that I never really processed. Every Expectation Hangover I experienced reactivated suppressed feelings, and because I didn't know how to move through them, my avoidance strategies kicked in. I distracted myself through work, numbed my feelings with food and television, or changed my prescription to a higher dose or different brand. It wasn't until my late twenties, when I learned how to process my emotions, that I was able to stop taking medication. (I am not asserting that antidepressants are not helpful or necessary; this is just my personal experience.)

You too have the courage to let go of your avoidance and suppression tactics, whatever they may be. It may feel scary, but I'll walk you through the process. I assure you that you will get through the darkness to the light — and it will be well worth it!

> "As a natural life force, emotions are intended to flow freely through our bodymind, then dissipate once we have fully experienced them and assimilated their valuable message."
> — Tim Brieske

HOW WE SUPPRESS EMOTIONS

Growing up, we learn how to add and subtract, read and write. Our parents teach us life skills like how to tie our shoes and drive a car. But how many of us are taught how to deal with our emotions effectively? We are told to "shake it off," "be a good girl/boy," "stop crying," that "it's not such a big deal," or that we are "overly sensitive." Because of the dismissive responses we receive and come to anticipate in others when strong emotions come up, our natural emotional responses feel wrong, shameful, or inappropriate. People in your life, especially your parents, while attempting to make you feel better or just being uncomfortable with strong emotions, taught you how to *not* fully experience emotions. Perhaps they jumped in to soothe you so you never learned how to fully feel a feeling. Or maybe they distracted you from the negative feeling by diverting your attention with a positive distraction such as candy or video games (hint: this is how addiction as a way to avoid and soothe emotions begins). Even if you had very loving parents, they may have interrupted the full expression of your feelings.

This isn't about blaming anyone. Everyone has always been doing the best they could with the tools they had. Chances are, your parents were not taught how to process emotions either. But it's up to you now to reverse the trend of suppression.

※ **EXERCISE**
Exploring Your Emotions

The first step in treating your Expectation Hangover on the emotional level is to become aware of how and when you began suppressing your feelings. This exercise will help you access a deeper understanding of your emotions. As you move through the following steps, answer each question in your journal. Begin writing (by hand) immediately after you read the question — don't stop to think about your answer. It doesn't matter if you don't remember a lot of specifics. Write anything that comes to mind; don't edit, analyze, or judge.

1. Find a quiet, comfortable place to sit where you won't be interrupted. Close your eyes for a moment and take yourself back to a
time in your childhood when you were really angry. Go with the
first memory that comes to mind; you can work through this process
again as other memories surface. After you have a memory, answer
these questions:

> What was the reaction of the people around you, such as your
> parents, siblings, peers, teachers, or coaches when you got
> angry?
> What were you told about being angry?
> What beliefs do you think you formed about expressing anger?

2. Repeat step 1 for each of the following feelings: sadness, fear, embarrassment, and excitement.
3. How did you see people in your family express their emotions?
4. What do you do today when you feel a big feeling (like anger, sadness, shame, fear, guilt, or excitement)? What do you tell yourself?
5. What avoidance strategies do you use to suppress your feelings?

Acknowledge yourself for having the courage to do this exercise. You
have now increased your awareness of how and when you began suppressing
your emotions. Take some time to reflect on this process in your journal.

. . . .

Emotions need a way to get out. If you do not express them, they will find
another exit! For instance, through over a decade of working with people
as a coach and spiritual counselor, I have noticed that unprocessed sadness
creates lethargy and even depression. Unexpressed anger can manifest in
irritability and anxiety. If you find yourself doing things like snapping at
a waiter, road raging, crying over things that you don't think should upset
you so much, constantly feeling "blah" and passionless, consistently looking
for external things to make you feel happy or peaceful, or using any of the
common quick-fix avoidance strategies, it is time to really face your feelings. *I understand it seems challenging, but suppressing and avoiding emotions is*

even harder work! The long-term drain on your energy from suppressing and avoiding your emotions is far greater than the short-term pain of acknowledging, feeling, and dealing with them.

Keeping your feelings inside is like attempting to hold an inflated beach ball under water. You can wrestle with it for a while; but sooner or later you lose your grasp on it, and it pops up, creating a huge splash and knocking you right in the face. If you have ever had a big feeling come up in a way that felt almost out of control, you know what I am talking about. During an Expectation Hangover it's common to have a disproportionate emotional reaction to a situation. You also may experience feelings that seem inappropriate or out of context. I remember being irritable and quite rude to my family when I was going through an Expectation Hangover regarding my career in my twenties (which makes sense because one of the symptoms of repressed anger is irritability). Although I recognized and didn't like that I was acting that way, I did not know how to change it until I learned how to process emotion.

Lynne met a man on a dating site and was excited about the potential she felt from their email and phone exchanges; but the morning of the date, he canceled. She was extremely disappointed, crying all the time, even though she didn't know this guy from Adam. She was questioning why this particular event upset her so much. What Lynne realized from her inflated emotional reaction to this dating experience was the following: "Feeling like no man wanted me goes back to feeling like my mother did not want me. It brought up all my childhood fears and sadness about not being good enough for my mom." At fifty-seven Lynne finally grieved the relationship she always longed for but never had with her mom. Since then, her life has turned around 180 degrees. Her business is flourishing, and she is experiencing causeless joy. "It is such a gift and a blessing to know that I can take care of myself emotionally. I don't *need* a man to take care of me anymore, and I do not get upset if I do not hear back from someone romantically. Now when a beloved comes into my life, I can share my life with him instead of needing his caretaking."

TRANSFORMATIONAL TRUTH
Creativity Is a Channel

During an Expectation Hangover many of us get creatively constipated. Negative emotions seem to sever the connection to our creative muse. But the muse is still there, and it is a healthy outlet for the painful feelings that come with disappointment. Think of some of your favorite songs, films, or pieces of art. Many were probably inspired by an Expectation Hangover; the artists channeled the rawness and realness of their pain into creating lyrics, stories, and images that touch our hearts.

Creative self-expression is important because it is one of the ways we can channel and release emotions. Use your anger or sadness to create something. Channel it into writing, painting, singing, or dancing. It doesn't matter if you are good at it or not.

I notice that people get depressed when they suppress their creativity. This is especially true for individuals who are highly right-brain oriented (inclined toward creativity) but grew up in very left-brain-oriented (logic-focused) environments. Since their creativity was often misunderstood and discouraged, they had to suppress it.

To get your creativity flowing, make time for it by putting it on your calendar. And just like you'd set the mood for a romantic evening, create an atmosphere for your creative process, using things like music, candles, and sacred objects. Create with enthusiasm, curiosity, and joy, but without attachment to the end product. Allow your emotions to come up and inspire you as you create. I have heard from many artists that there are teardrops in their paintings.

Do not judge yourself or attempt to edit your expression while you are creating it. Doing so will only interrupt your process and shift you away from the emotional part of your brain to the analytical part (and don't you spend enough time there anyway?). After you create something, acknowledge yourself for it! Celebrating — not evaluating — is key to honoring your self-expression.

ROLE-PLAYING Rx: THE SURFER

"I used to fight the pain, but recently this became clear to me:
pain is not my enemy. It is my call to greatness.
Learning about what you're made of is always time well spent."
— Henry Rollins

It is time for some role-playing Rx. The role you are going to take on to treat the emotional level of your Expectation Hangover is that of the Surfer. Even if you have never surfed before, you know the basic principles of surfing. A surfer paddles out into the ocean completely willing to face the waves. He has no control over the ocean or the wave that comes in, but he does have a choice over how he responds to it. The surfer must be present, allow the wave to carry him, and rely on his surfing skills to keep him safe. A good surfer knows that if he attempts to avoid, overpower, or swim against a wave, he will never experience the exhilaration and freedom that come from riding the wave all the way through. Think of the waves as your emotions and your surfing skills as the processes you'll be learning in this chapter.

By taking on the role of the Surfer, you will become skilled at riding the emotional waves of your Expectation Hangover, which include all the feelings you have avoided and suppressed up to now. You will realize that your emotions, just like waves, have peaks but gradually subside, landing you softly on the beach, where you are free from the emotional symptoms of your Expectation Hangover.

I recently received this email from Lola:

I thought my future involved being a mother and a wife. Fast-forward to the present, and I'm divorced, dithering about a career, worrying about money, living in the spare room of a kind relative's house, and wondering what the hell I'm going to do. For almost two years now, I have been exhausted, stressed, unmotivated. Chocolate has become a daily food group. I feel a lot of toxic emotions brewing — resentment, guilt, bitterness, blame, sadness — and it can be quite seductive to just let them take me over and indulge in the "woe is me" thoughts. How can I stay afloat when it feels like such a struggle?

Relief will not come from attempting to stay afloat, as if you were holding on to a small life preserver and being bounced around by the waves. The Surfer rides each wave of emotion — no matter how big or scary — without any judgment, analysis, or desire to get out of the situation. Probably the best illustration of this is a child's temper tantrum, which goes something like this: The child gets upset about something. The emotion escalates, usually to anger and frustration. Then the tears and sobbing begin as sadness and disappointment well up. There may be a few waves of these emotions. Eventually, if the child is given the time and space to feel all the feelings, the emotions begin to subside, exhaustion hits, and the child begins to whimper. Acceptance sets in, and the child begins rocking or curling up into a ball (forms of self-soothing). Finally, the child nurtures him- or herself out of being upset and heads back to playing. Before avoidance strategies set it, children are natural surfers of their emotions!

Now, it's important to note that the child usually does not get to the other side of a temper tantrum if someone comes in and tries to stop it. Similarly, it is impossible for us to get to peace and acceptance if we interrupt our feelings before fully expressing them. Processing emotion means allowing ourselves to fully experience all our emotions just like a child having a temper tantrum. In a tool I will share a bit later, you will learn how to have an adult version of a temper tantrum that will guide you through the trajectory of an emotional experience in a healthy way.

At forty-seven Jack was suffering an Expectation Hangover from a layoff, and an entrepreneurial experience that went sour had him panicked about his next step. After our first meeting I wondered whether he would come back to see me, as I was certain he left with an Expectation Hangover about our session. You see, Jack came in dead set on my helping him get his résumé in order and "figure out" what he was going to do. He was tense, down, and rather short tempered. I told him I really could not help him until he dealt with some of his feelings about his Expectation Hangover, to which he responded, "I'm *fine*. I just need to get a job, and I'll feel better." Yet I knew that emotional beach ball Jack was holding under water was preventing him from moving forward. Jack believed that coping strategies like being strong and distracting himself were better than feeling. I asked if he would be willing to do a specific kind of journaling that is a treatment tool on the emotional level (you'll learn this tool a bit later), before our next meeting. Reluctantly, he said yes. I gave him some sentence stems that I knew would trigger emotion and sent him on his way.

The next week, Jack reported that in his journaling, a lot of shame and sadness came up that he had no idea he was hanging on to. The next few sessions were dedicated to giving Jack the space to express his feelings. He talked about the shame and intense sadness he felt over his perceived failure. Tears ran down Jack's face, and the gift of his Expectation Hangover was revealed. For the first time since he was a very little boy, he actually cried. This release opened up so much space for Jack that he felt he got his confidence and energy back.

By honoring his own feelings, Jack felt a sense of worthiness he had not felt in a while. As he was able to take on the role of the Surfer and use the techniques you will learn in this chapter, he released shame he had been carrying around for years. His entire approach to his career shifted from a place of desperation to a place where he saw how much he had to offer. Within two months, he had a new job offer that came from an old colleague who called him "out of the blue," and he is thriving in his new position.

Many of us avoid diving into the sea of our emotions because we are afraid we will fall into a black hole of despair and pain that we cannot climb out of. But every surfer has a sturdy board that he is always connected to through a surf leash (a cord that connects his ankle to the board so that even if he falls off and feels separated from the board, he never loses his connection to it). The board you are always connected to as you surf the waves of your emotions is your own compassion. H. Ronald Hulnick and Mary R. Hulnick have defined healing as "the application of Loving to the places inside that hurt." We apply this love by being compassionate with ourselves.

Let's examine the word *compassion* and its roots, *co*, which means "with," and *passion*, which means "suffering." *Compassion* basically means being "with suffering." One reason counseling and coaching are so powerful is that they offer a safe space for the client to express feelings while receiving loving compassion from the counselor or coach. Your own compassion will keep you safe. You can even think of this part of you as an unconditionally loving and nurturing parent who gives you permission and encouragement to express your feelings fully. You may not always experience the connection to this part of yourself, but trust me — it's there!

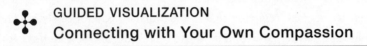

GUIDED VISUALIZATION
Connecting with Your Own Compassion

You can download the audio version of this exercise at
www.expectationhangover.com/bonus

The Surfer is aware there is a part of us that is experiencing the emotion and another part of us that is simply with us, offering us compassion. This visualization exercise will help you become aware of and connect to your own self-compassion. Read all the directions so you understand them, then take yourself through the exercise.

1. Find a quiet, comfortable place to sit where you won't be interrupted. Close your eyes, take three deep, slow breaths, and bring yourself into the present moment.

2. Repeat, inwardly or aloud, the affirmation "I am choosing to be with myself in this moment" and take another deep breath.

3. Bring your awareness to someone you love very much and for whom you have a tremendous amount of compassion. No matter what they do or don't do, no matter what they are going through, you love them and feel compassion toward them. You can be with their suffering. It can be a person or a pet. Choose someone you accept unconditionally, and really visualize that person in your mind's eye.

4. Notice the feelings that come up as you bring that person into your awareness. Feel the love and compassion you are experiencing. Experience seeing through the eyes of love.

5. Now take all the love, compassion, and acceptance you are experiencing as you think of that person and direct it toward yourself. See yourself in your mind's eye being surrounded by your own love. You

can visualize this love as a soft lavender or pink color that is wrapping itself around you like a warm blanket. See yourself through eyes of love. This is compassion.

6. Notice how it feels to be connecting to the part of you that unconditionally loves and has an infinite amount of compassion.

7. Anchor this experience by bringing your hand to your heart. Take another deep breath and inhale love. Exhale a sigh of relief. Now that you have this reference point, you can always connect to your own self-compassion by bringing your hand to your heart.

8. When you are ready, slowly open your eyes and bring your awareness back into the room.

9. Take some time to reflect on this process in your journal.

. . . .

Recycling versus Releasing Feelings

"If you want to enjoy the rainbow, be prepared to endure the storm."
— Warren Wendel Wiersbe

Now, you may be thinking, "I'm an emotional person. I do feel my feelings — I cry, and sometimes I even yell." Or, "I've processed my emotions in the past. There is no deep emotional work I need to do related to my hangover." Did you have a good cry yet still get limited relief, despite going through a box of Kleenex? Or take your anger to a boxing class but still leave feeling mad about something? Or experience temporary relief from upsetting emotions tied to Expectation Hangovers in the past but notice that they tend to resurface in a familiar way when another disappointment comes along? These things happen because most of us *recycle* our feelings rather than truly *releasing* them.

Without self-compassion (remember self-compassion is the lifeline the Surfer relies on when riding the waves of emotion), the same feeling continues to get triggered in different ways. I call this recycling. Conversely, releasing a feeling is when you allow yourself to express it without any judgment, analysis, interpretation, or desire to get out of it. Feelings get recycled rather than released when we try to interpret, blame, figure out, or fix them rather than allowing them to be expressed. When we do not allow ourselves to become the Surfer and ride the feeling long enough to experience its full impact, we end up recycling the feeling, and it continues to resurface.

The hangover-like symptoms we experience and the judgments we make are usually connected to unresolved issues from the past with a similar resonance. It's as if some part of our consciousness is saying, "Oh, I feel a sense of rejection right now. Hmmm . . . I've felt this before. So now I'm going to bring up all those familiar feelings from the past that are still inside because maybe now that they've been triggered again, I can heal them." For example, during my divorce, I was processing not only the end of the relationship with my husband, but also the unprocessed grief from my earlier life that I had pushed aside. This cumulative experience is the way all Expectation Hangovers work, which is why they can feel so emotionally overwhelming and confusing.

> "Feelings or emotions are the universal language and are to be honored.
> They are the authentic expression of who you are at your deepest place."
> — Judith Wright

After Lindsay's sudden breakup with her boyfriend of three years, she was overwhelmed with grief over the loss of the man she thought was "the one." She lost weight, was not motivated to go out, and felt like crying every day. On the advice of friends and out of her own desire to get over her ex, she threw her skinny jeans back on and jumped right into dating. About five months after her breakup, she met Chris. He wined her, dined her, and told her how fabulous she was. This felt so much better than sitting at home crying about the other guy. A year later they were engaged. Yet a few months after her wedding, she came to me complaining about how much anxiety she felt about his work travel schedule. Chris spent about three days on the road each week. While he was away, Lindsay felt panicked; but when he got back home, she wasn't that interested in her brand-new husband. "I don't get why I feel so anxious and sad. I have everything I want in my life. What is going on?" The very thing that was supposed to make her happy simply wasn't.

Lindsay shared with me that her father left her family when she was seven years old. She felt sad and abandoned but did not express her feelings because she saw how upset her mom was and wanted to be strong for her. As a little girl, Lindsay learned how to put on a mask and pretend she was fine. She distracted herself from her sadness by focusing on her schoolwork and taking care of her mom. When her boyfriend broke up with her, which felt similar to the rejection and abandonment she felt when her dad left, she suppressed her sadness just as she did when she was a young girl. Now that the shininess of her newest relationship had worn off and her husband's frequent travel was triggering her abandonment issues once again, the feelings of sadness about her previous boyfriend and all the grief and sadness she had repressed and recycled throughout her life came up.

The more we try to get out of feeling our feelings, the more baggage we are storing up. So you might as well open the floodgates now; otherwise there will just be some other Expectation Hangover in the future in which the Universe will invite you to do the same thing again. In Lindsay's case, she stopped avoiding the pain and was willing to go back to painful moments in her life. After working with the powerful tools of the Surfer, Lindsay was able to let go of old hurts and open her heart fully to her husband. Today she is happily in love and recently gave birth to her first son.

※ **EXERCISE**
Uncovering Recycled Feelings

This exercise will help you bring unresolved issues into your consciousness. You will take an even deeper look into the emotions you are experiencing to find those that have been repressed in the past and that are being recycled into your current Expectation Hangover. Get out your journal and move through the following steps. For this exercise you will need to refer back to your Expectation Hangover Assessment Form (p. 28).

1. Find a quiet, comfortable place to sit where you won't be inter-rupted. Refer back to your answer to question 5 on the Expectation Hangover Assessment Form ("What feelings are you experienc-ing?") and elaborate on your answer, using the sentence stem "This Expectation Hangover makes me feel..."

2. Refer back to your answer to question 12 on the Expectation Hang-over Assessment Form ("Does this Expectation Hangover remind you of things from your past? Are certain memories surfacing? How does this feel familiar?") and expand on your answer, using the fol-lowing sentence stems:

> I have felt like this before when...
> This reminds me of...
> I remember when...

Be sure to write as much as you can for each sentence stem. Allow the memories to flow.

3. Take some time to reflect on this process in your journal.

You now have a better understanding of the thread that ties together feelings from cumulative Expectation Hangovers, and you are even more prepared to release your emotions.

. . . .

"It's about just really, really feeling it and honoring it,
knowing it is a very important part of humanness.
When I relax into pain, instead of pushing it away, it melts."
— Elizabeth Lesser

Now that you have some context for what riding the waves of your emo-tions means and have tapped into self-compassion, you are ready to dive in and fully release your feelings. Once again you call on the Surfer, but this time you are willing to go much farther out in the ocean and catch a much bigger wave. Not only are you willing to express feelings about your current Expectation Hangover; you are going to fully experience them. I am going to share with you the two most effective tools I have found for releasing feel-ings: release writing and the temper tantrum technique.

⟡ **TOOL**
Release Writing

Release writing is much different from journaling because it is more "stream of consciousness" in approach. Unlike journaling, where you are writing in a slower, more thoughtful way to allow interpretation and reflection, release writing is really a process of dumping. Just like a surfer, who cannot control the flow of the wave he is on (or another wave that may come in), do not attempt to control your feelings by editing or pausing to reflect.

When using this technique, write by hand, not on a computer, because release writing is a kinesthetic activity. You write with the intention of keeping up with the pace of your thoughts. Although it may be challenging to keep up with the speed of your emerging thoughts and feelings, write as fast as you can so you do not miss the wave that is coming in. You probably won't finish writing a sentence before another sensation or thought comes up. Don't worry about spelling, punctuation, or the legibility of what you are writing. Keep writing until you experience a sense of relief and emptiness. Upon completion, burn or rip up the paper to release the energy. Do not interpret, analyze, or go back to read what you wrote, because that would only recycle your emotions. The purpose of this process is to embody the Surfer and ride the waves of what you are experiencing so that emotions you may have suppressed or avoided can begin to flow.

There are two ways you can use the release-writing process. The first is to use it when you feel really upset by your Expectation Hangover. Instead of avoiding or suppressing your emotions, grab some paper and just begin to write. Allow yourself to really feel the emotions as you write, and continue until the intensity of the feeling decreases to a point where you feel relief. The second way is to make a practice of this technique by committing to a minimum of ten minutes of release writing per day for at least forty days. Spiritual experts and scientists agree that it takes forty days to create a new habit — the time it takes to form new neural pathways in the brain. If you commit to using this process as a way to release emotions, I assure you that you will purge yourself of a lot of recycled emotions you have been carrying around for decades. If forty days feels like too much, simply committing to using this tool to help you release the emotions that are being triggered by your Expectation Hangover is a great start. Release writing was inspired by and adapted from the free-form writing technique developed by John-Roger and the Movement of Spiritual Inner Awareness.

. . . .

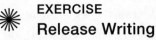

EXERCISE
Release Writing

For this exercise you will need two or three sheets of blank, lined paper, a pen that is very comfortable and easy to write with, a candle, and a timer. When you do this exercise, it is essential that you write by hand.

1. Find a quiet, comfortable place to sit where you won't be interrupted, and set a timer for ten minutes. You can keep writing after the timer ends, but the minimum is ten minutes. Remember, emotions are like waves — they have peaks and valleys — so support your expressive process by giving yourself plenty of time to ride the waves.

2. Before you begin, light the candle and ask, "May only that which is for my Highest Good come forward."

3. Take a moment to connect to your Higher Self by bringing your hand to your heart. Feel this unconditionally loving and compassionate part of you. This is your surfboard and will keep you safe as you ride the waves of your emotions.

4. Beginning writing. Just write whatever comes to you. Whatever you do, keep writing. Don't stop. Even if all you can write is "I don't know what to write." Use these sentence stems to prompt you if you need them, but do not feel that you have to follow a script:

> I'm angry because...
> I'm sad because...
> I'm ashamed because...
> I'm disappointed because...
> I'm scared because...
> I feel guilty because...

Do not edit yourself. Do not interpret or analyze. Do not try to make sense of it or make it legible. Just let it rip! This is your opportunity to let it all out. If tears come, allow yourself to cry. Whatever you do, keep riding the waves of your emotions. Don't stop.

5. At the end of the ten minutes, if you feel that you're done, you can move to the next step. If you feel there is still emotion present, keep writing.

6. When you're done writing, take a moment and bring your hand to your heart. Take in a nice, deep breath and connect to the love inside you. Acknowledge yourself for your courage and willingness to work through this exercise.

7. Take the paper (do not attempt to reread it!) and either rip it up in tiny pieces or burn it. You do this to fully release the energy. Then wash your hands up to your elbows.

8. Take some time to reflect on this process in your journal. Since release writing is such a cleansing process, big realizations often come up afterward.

· · · ·

BETH'S STORY

The hardest part of my unexpected job loss was being with all the feelings that came up. There were moments when I felt so lost, so out of control and confused. I was afraid that I wouldn't find work again. I felt like a huge failure. The best thing I did to treat my Expectation Hangover was to allow the bigness of all my feelings to come out. I could not force them out on command, but I did my best not to suppress them. I did not avoid them, and I did not numb them. I trusted that the process I was going through was just that — a process. It had to play out. I was patient and gentle with myself rather than blaming myself or thinking that I could have prevented it. In the past I had used drugs, alcohol, food, and sex as ways to escape the feelings. But this time I faced the storm head-on, and I surfed the waves of my emotions. I learned about my own strength, and my capacity for tolerating my own discomfort increased the more I practiced. That time in my life came with so much pain, but it also was some of my greatest learning. It altered the trajectory of my self-discovery. It's a huge part of who I am today — and it really prepared me for the job I now have, which I love!

TOOL
Temper Tantrum Technique

Using the role-playing Rx of the Surfer, this tool will support you in the full release of your emotion similar to how a child has a temper tantrum. I understand that this technique may seem unusual, but from both my own life and my work with thousands of clients and workshop participants, I know how powerful and purifying it is. Keep an open mind and trust the wisdom of your childhood expression. We all knew how to express our feelings as children before we became self-conscious and adopted avoidance and suppression strategies. In this technique you give yourself full permission to bring up negative feelings. You allow yourself to feel angry, scared, ashamed, and so on. You welcome the feelings to come up in their fullest expression. It is okay to yell and cry — in fact, it is often essential to our healing. Expectation Hangovers prepare us to go through an apparently impenetrable wall, and the intense feelings concerning this wall are the very fuel that will propel you through it. These feelings are the access to your hidden power and potential.

Remember that if your feelings begin to feel big and scary, that you are always connected to your own self-compassion. There is a part of you that is feeling big feelings and a part of you that is keeping you safe by holding a loving space ready for you.

. . . .

EXERCISE
Temper Tantrum Technique

For this exercise you will need a candle, a large pillow, some Kleenex, your journal, and a stuffed animal if you have one.

1. Find a quiet, comfortable place to sit where you won't be interrupted. Make sure it's a place where you'll have privacy.

2. Before you begin, light the candle and ask, "May only that which is for my Highest Good come forward."

3. Take a moment to connect to your Higher Self by bringing your hand to your heart. Feel this unconditionally loving and compassionate part of you. This is your surfboard and will keep you safe as you ride the waves of your emotions.

4. Take some time to think about your Expectation Hangover and what is really upsetting you. Saying what you are upset about out loud is a great way to begin bringing your feelings to the surface. Use sentence starters like these:

   > I'm mad because...
   > I'm sad because...
   > I'm hurt because...
   > This sucks because...

5. Let the emotions come up. Resist the temptation to analyze your feelings or the situation that is triggering them.

6. Allow yourself the full experience of the feeling, keeping an open body position. If anger comes up and you want to hit the pillow in front of you, go for it! Or if you want to, scream into it. If there are tears, let yourself cry. Instead of contracting your body and looking down, keep your head up and your chest open, and ride the waves of what you are feeling.

"I have been allowing myself to feel the loss, the pain, the sadness, and the anger from this Expectation Hangover. I am being patient and gentle with myself, not blaming myself for doing anything wrong or thinking that I could have prevented it. The more I allow myself to just feel, the better I feel."

— April

7. Continue tuning in to your Higher Self for words of encouragement. The most important part of releasing a feeling is to have compassion for yourself the entire time you are going through it. Gently say to yourself, "It's okay. Let that out. You are doing great. Keep going." Continue riding the waves of your feelings just as you did during a temper tantrum when you were a child.

8. As you start to feel the intensity of your emotions decreasing, it is important to engage in self-soothing of some kind. You may feel like rocking a bit, putting your arms around yourself, or curling up with your pillow or a stuffed animal.

9. Spend some time nurturing yourself and just being with yourself. Then imagine yourself as a surfer safely and gently arriving on a beautiful beach.

10. Take three deep, slow breaths. Put your hand back on your heart and fill yourself with love. Acknowledge yourself for your courage and willingness to work through this exercise.

11. Take some time to reflect on this process in your journal.

· · · ·

BUT I'M NOT ANGRY!

"Holding on to anger is like grasping a hot coal with the intent of throwing it at someone else; you are the one who gets burned."
— Buddha

Anger. We are all angry. Yes, even you. It is the emotion I find we avoid the most or process the most incorrectly. Anger comes up frequently during an Expectation Hangover, as we often feel blindsided, wronged, or frustrated — so leverage this opportunity to release a powerful emotion! Underneath anger is passion. If you want to feel more passionate about life, you have to feel your anger first. You cannot get to the fiery, passionate part of you without expressing that anger first. Anger is especially important for women to express since, as little girls, we are not really "allowed" to have this emotion. But men have a lot of repressed or misdirected anger as well. The bottom line is that it is crucial for all of us to get it out in a healthy way.

Anger is scary; I get that. But what is more terrifying is keeping it inside, where it can transform into irritability, criticism, judgment, and even illness. Anger is a very active energy, so it will either find a way out in one of those forms or be directed at someone — either ourselves or someone else. I want to emphasize that expressing anger at someone else directly to their face is not a healthy way to release it. Instead, take that anger into a temper tantrum process or release writing, where you can get it out *about* them but not *at* them. You can be angry at anyone else, including God, but please don't ever direct your anger inward. This is a form of self-beating that is not therapeutic. You can be angry *about* being frustrated with yourself, which isn't the same as being angry *at* yourself. For example, telling yourself, "I'm so angry that I'm so hard on myself" or "I hate not being nice to myself" is being angry *about* something that is upsetting. But telling yourself, "I'm a loser," "I'm a failure," or "I'm so mad at myself" is being angry *at* yourself. See the difference?

Vikki came to one of my workshops with the intention of getting over a breakup with a man who was emotionally unavailable yet whom she still yearned to be with. Vikki told me that she was not angry about anything. That she had forgiven her own and others' past wrongs and did not feel mad about anything. However, her irritability and attachment to her ex were clues that she was holding on to unprocessed anger. I sensed that there was a tremendous breakthrough available to her if she was willing to actually go to the depths of her raw, real emotions using the temper tantrum technique. I challenged her assertion that she was "over things," trusting that if she gave herself access to the well of anger inside her, a huge release would be possible. And was it ever!

Thanks to her own courage and the collective energy of all the participants going through the exercise at the same time, Vikki tapped into her anger. She hit, screamed, cried — riding all the waves of her emotions with a rawness that was inspiring. When she had tapped into her unexpressed emotions, a lot of anger toward her father, who had passed away ten years earlier, came up. She cried tears that she had been holding inside for decades. After the exercise, she looked lighter and brighter than ever before. In a meditation shortly after this process, she was visited by her father's spirit and received a very personal message from him that led to a level of forgiveness she had never experienced before. Her Expectation Hangover about her relationship dissolved because she was able to see it was just a catalyst for facing the emotions she was holding on to regarding her father. This is the power of the temper tantrum technique.

THE POWER OF VULNERABILITY

"Staying vulnerable is a risk we have to take
if we want to experience connection."
— Brené Brown

Being raw and real in front of others is another important part of healing your Expectation Hangover on the emotional level. Just as there are times when surfing is a solitary process, there are other times when being part of a surfing community is valuable for support, encouragement, and positive reinforcement. Riding the waves of our emotions alone can get lonely and prevents us from receiving the healing energy of compassion from others. Anything we keep inside because we judge it as dark is transformed the moment we bring it into the light. In moments of vulnerability, where we are being fully authentic by sharing our innermost experience, healing can occur.

JASMINE'S STORY

My twelve-year-old daughter deals with depression, anxiety, and behavioral issues. Many kids don't understand her, and she has been bullied a lot, despite my attempts to protect her. Because of the shame I felt over (as I saw it) failing as a mother, I gained a lot of weight and withdrew from friendships, as it was too hard to go out and pretend I was happy and had perfect children when it wasn't the truth. Being honest with myself that I'm not perfect and I don't have a perfect daughter has been hard, as I've always been a perfectionist. I thought of myself as a failure at home, so I put my heart and soul into my job. I would hide my sadness and come to work as though I were an actress and just play the "perfect teacher" role. My friends and family had no idea, and I was living a lie.

Eventually, I couldn't take the charade anymore, so I let people see my vulnerable side. As scary as it was to drop the facade, it was even more liberating. I began to open up to others and let my feelings show, which made my students, colleagues, friends, and strangers identify with me more. This experience taught me not to worry what my neighbors or other people think of me or my daughter or my parenting skills. My heart has softened by letting people see the real me, and now it is easy for me to see that my daughter has a heart of gold and that I'll always be her number one fan, no matter what. We are now closer, as I have lowered my expectations of us both, and now she is free to be the quirky, lovable yet anxious, and sometimes sad and vulnerable young lady she is.

Shame often stands as the guard at the gate to vulnerability. The incredibly painful feeling of shame is based on a misunderstanding of a perceived flaw that we believe must stay hidden. The way to get through shame is by stepping into vulnerability and revealing what we are terrified of being "found out" for. We all want to know that we are loved "even if" we have these dark, scary, shameful feelings and thoughts.

Josh is transgendered, meaning he was biologically born a female but felt he was trapped in the wrong body. He was not able to express himself fully, which affected all areas of his life and led to many Expectation Hangovers. He was consistently made fun of and felt ashamed. He settled for less than he wanted or deserved, allowing people to walk all over him. He was surviving, not living. Then came a time when he couldn't handle it anymore, and he sought professional help. Josh came out to a few friends and got an amazing amount of support. That gave him the courage to come out to family and close friends, where he was met with acceptance and love. Josh says, "I'm practicing self-expression at a new level. I'm learning vulnerability; the importance of living and sharing one's truth; and how blessed I am to know what it is like to have experienced life in both genders and to be able to share my gifts with others."

TRANSFORMATIONAL TRUTH
Authenticity over Strategy

To avoid being hurt, we manage the expression of our true feelings so we feel safe. Often we become so attached to what another person will think, say, or do that we become overly strategic rather than being truly authentic. We can discount vulnerability because it just feels too risky. But we cannot truly experience the delicious emotions that a relationship offers if we are not authentic. I invite you to read the word intimacy as "into-me-see." We create intimacy with others when we allow ourselves to be seen. Vulnerability is our way out of avoiding emotion for fear of how it will be received.

Exposing our deepest feelings in the presence of another person may seem scary. Where strategy is useful is in choosing whom to share with. It needs to be someone who will not judge you, advise you, or attempt to interrupt your process. This person can be a dear friend, family member, mentor, coach, or counselor who will be able to receive the gift of your vulnerability with compassion. I encourage you to create the context for sharing an authentic conversation by asking if the other person is willing to just listen. You can also request that they do not offer any advice unless you specifically ask for it. Revealing your vulnerability is not about problem solving; it is about exposing and releasing.

As you practice vulnerability with others whom you choose, share from your heart, not your head. Surf whatever emotions arise, by letting yourself cry. Ride waves of anger or frustration by not restraining your voice or editing your words. Tell them the secrets you've locked away because you've been too ashamed to speak them aloud. Allow yourself to express the range of your emotions — go for full authenticity. Let yourself be messy. Forget about grammar, making sense, or looking pretty while you cry. Be free with your expression. If you feel nervous or ashamed, I suggest expressing it by saying, "I feel ashamed" or "I'm nervous about sharing this." Remember, the key ingredients of vulnerability are authenticity and intimacy. State what is and let yourself be seen!

Vulnerability is required for us to connect to each other on the deepest level. Think of someone you feel very close to. My guess is that there have been times when you have shared a feeling with that person that felt risky to expose; yet when it was received with love rather than judgment, your relationship got stronger. I have learned that my own vulnerability is a great strength and has largely contributed to my internal healing as well as my external success. When I removed the expectations I had of myself to achieve and began really allowing people to see me — the real me, not the "I've got it all together" me — everything in my life began to shift. My relationships became a lot richer because vulnerability is a currency that makes us wealthy in love and connection. The more I get emotionally naked with the people in my life, the closer I feel to them and the more resources I have to turn to when I am feeling the emotional symptoms of an Expectation Hangover.

Vulnerability was what helped me move out of my Expectation Hangover regarding my career. By sharing my own story and exposing my feelings, I have been able to write books and create content that people resonate with. It is a great gift we give to another person when we let them see behind any masks or walls of emotional protection. Moreover, vulnerability is a priceless gift to give to yourself.

> "There's really nothing I wouldn't share. You're only as sick as your secrets,
> and I don't have any secrets. I'll talk about anything.
> I want to be part of the conversation that breaks down shame."
> — Seane Corn

MAKE A DATE WITH YOUR FEELINGS

Since feelings sometimes come up at inconvenient times, like in the middle of your workday or when other people are around, you may not always be able to address them immediately. Yet you need a way to respond to them that does not perpetuate suppression and avoidance. And I have a great way for you to do that: you get to make a date with your feelings! When you experience a negative feeling, instead of attempting to ignore it or make it go away, simply acknowledge it in the moment. You do this by inwardly saying to the feeling, "Hello [insert whatever feeling is present]. I feel, acknowledge, and honor your presence. I know you have an important message for me, and I commit to dealing with you at [insert a time you know you will be alone and available to fully feel your feeling]."

Do not flake out on your date with your feelings! Keeping your word with yourself is an important part of building self-trust; and self-trust is an integral part of feeling confident in your ability to move through the emotional level of an Expectation Hangover. Our feelings have feelings. I know that may sound strange, but it's true. When our feelings don't feel they are acknowledged, they end up being recycled and coming back later, snowballing into a more intense feeling, or even manifesting as a health issue, to try and get our attention in another way. So honor them because they always present an opportunity for learning and healing.

CONCLUSION

Whew — what a ride! I understand that surfing the waves of your emotions is not exactly comfortable or easy, so I truly applaud you for being willing to dive in. You now have some powerful techniques in your toolbox for identifying, expressing, and releasing your feelings. If you find yourself tempted to suppress or avoid, I encourage you to call upon your inner Surfer even if the waves look rough and you think you'd be more comfortable on the beach. Being able to process your emotions is not only integral to treating your Expectation Hangover; it is key to your overall well-being.

E-motion is energy in motion. It needs to move in order to be expressed. If you are feeling overwhelmed about how to change an intense emotional reaction, remember that simply realizing that you have the *choice* about how to respond to it stops the recycling! Sometimes you just need to write, scream, hit a pillow, sob — with *no* judgment or analysis — or have a big laugh about it! Give yourself permission to have an adult temper tantrum. You can also express your emotions by moving your body through exercising or dancing (my favorite!). Or take that emotional energy and channel it into something creative, like painting, cooking, or writing. We *all* have feelings, and they need a forum for expression. And the more you surf the waves of your emotions, the more skilled at it you become. Soon the waves will not feel so big or scary.

> "When you feel your emotions, you begin discovering what is truly important to you. When you honor what is important to you, you begin to live authentically."
> — Marianne Williamson

Chapter Seven

THE MENTAL LEVEL

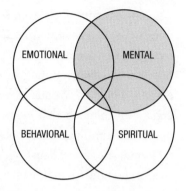

"Thought. It's at the heart of everything we experience, from monsters to angels and from problems to possibilities. And since we have an infinite potential for new thought, we're only ever one new thought away from a completely different experience of being alive."

— Michael Neill

Think about the thoughts you have during an Expectation Hangover. Are they positive, uplifting, and calming? Do they keep you in the present moment? Are you able to direct them and quiet them? Are they kind, empowering, and supportive? The answer to these questions is most likely no. Our mind either takes us to a past we want to change or to a future we are worried about. And it can be challenging, or seemingly impossible, to redirect our mind.

Your experience directly follows your thoughts; therefore your mind can be your best ally or your worst enemy. Our brain is actually more wired for negativity because thousands of years ago, our focus was primarily on survival and our minds needed to anticipate bad things that could happen. Even though we have evolved beyond a primary focus on survival, our mind defaults to negative when an Expectation Hangover comes along and we feel uncertainty. However, it is possible to rewire our brains in a way that produces a higher ratio of life-affirming thoughts to negative ones. Even though things may feel out of your control during an Expectation Hangover, your thoughts are something you actually *do* have dominion over. But this is easy to forget because during an Expectation Hangover, a lot feels out of control.

Not knowing feels even scarier when everything you thought was true does not feel true anymore. To get the certainty we crave, our mind takes over, but not necessarily in a good way: We obsess over what did or didn't happen, constantly tuning in to the same mental frequencies of "shoulda, coulda, woulda." We judge ourselves and engage in negative self-talk. We engage in thinking that creates guilt, regret, fear, anxiety, and worry. We perpetuate limiting beliefs because we are not sure what is true. These mental gymnastics are exhausting, and you can move beyond them! This chapter focuses on how to think in a way that alleviates suffering on the mental level during an Expectation Hangover.

YOUR STORY

"Beliefs have the power to create and the power to destroy. Human beings have the awesome ability to take any experience of their lives and create a meaning that disempowers them or one that can literally save their lives."
— Tony Robbins

All Expectation Hangovers come from having expectations, and where are expectations created? That's right — in your mind! Thanks to your suffering, you now have the willingness to reprogram your mind and release expectations, but first you need to understand how it got programmed. The vast majority of what and how we think is based on a story we have about ourselves, others, and how life works. We began to construct this story at a young age, based on things we saw, heard, or experienced. We formed judgments about what happened, and then those judgments created clusters of thoughts. The thoughts then created a belief system containing expectations about ourselves, others, and life in general. Over the years, I have heard some pretty atrocious stories that people honestly believe about themselves: "I am too damaged for a man to want me." "I am a wreck in relationships." "I'm just not good." "I fail at most things, and I have the résumé to prove it." "I don't think I really deserve money." "I have to work really hard to get anything I desire." "Everyone else is better than me." And that is just a small sampling.

Our story becomes the lens through which we start to see everything in our life, and we tend to attract circumstances that fit with our story — even if we don't consciously want them — because we expect them. You'll notice that many of the Expectation Hangovers you are experiencing fit perfectly with your story. For example, if you were teased, you probably created a story about being "less than" (this was a big part of my own story), and your Expectation Hangover may have something to do with being rejected or feeling separate. If you were abandoned, you likely have a story about being unlovable, and your Expectation Hangovers may have to do with heartache or someone leaving. If you were poor, you possibly have a story about being undeserving, and your Expectation Hangovers may have to do with challenges in generating abundance in your life in the areas of money, relationships, career opportunities, and/or health. If you have a story about being a victim, you may find yourself in a variety of Expectation Hangovers that you judge as unfair or that make you feel you were wronged. The beliefs that make up our story become the operating system that determines the way we think and, consequently, what we tend to attract and experience in our lives.

"When I was launching my business, I felt torn between thoughts that got me excited about my vision and thoughts that completely sabotaged me, which came from being terrified of bearing responsibility for the destinies of the people who would be counting on me to lead them. It was a risky venture, so I was unconsciously reverting to past conditioning because my parents were intellectuals who always reinforced the need to be realistic and pragmatic. I learned that between the time we set an intention and the time we send it out with expectation, a lot of counterintentions pop up. They pop up in order to be released; they are actually just signals that in order to create something new, we have to get rid of old baggage."

— Tabitha

TRANSFORMATIONAL TRUTH
The Problem with the Law of Attraction

Perhaps you have heard of the law of attraction, which states that "like attracts like" and that by focusing on positive or negative thoughts, one can bring about positive or negative results. The common flaw in our understanding of this law is that we believe all we have to do is think about or visualize something to manifest it. It is true that we attract at the level of our own vibration and that our thoughts and words are extremely magnetic. But the most powerful attractor is our belief system. You can create beautiful poster boards full of images of what you want and affirm every day that you are available for an incredibly successful, passionate career or a loving relationship; but if you don't truly believe you are enough, worthy, lovable, and deserving, then attracting a great career or relationship into your life may be more challenging. Consider what limiting beliefs you have that contradict your desires and upgrade them to beliefs that are in alignment with what you want to attract.

I am not saying this to make you think you have created all your disappointment, but rather to empower you with an understanding of your story and how it influences your life. Your Expectation Hangover could be the very thing that is making you uncomfortable enough to change your mind about what you choose to believe and therefore attract. But how does one become aware of what has been a completely habitual way of thinking? It begins with an investigation of the thoughts that have become your story.

> "What happens is of little significance compared with
> the stories we tell ourselves about what happens.
> Events matter little, only stories of events affect us."
> — Rabih Alameddine

 EXERCISE
Your Storyboard

Before you can create new results in your life, you need to get familiar with the old story you have been carrying around like a heavy backpack for decades. When we buy into the beliefs of our story, we are buying into misunderstandings that perpetuate Expectation Hangovers on the mental level. Breaking free of your story takes conscious attention. To do this, you are going to investigate your personal storyboard.

1. Find a quiet, comfortable place to sit where you won't be interrupted. Begin by making a time line of your life. Draw a horizontal line across a sheet of paper and write "Birth" at the far left and "Today" at the far right.

2. On the line, mark down significant life events that were challenging for you and the corresponding age. For example: "Age 6 = Parents divorce," "Age 14 = First broken heart," "Age 18 = Did not get into college of choice." These events are where most of your limiting beliefs come from.

3. For each significant event, list the beliefs you formed because of the event. For example: "Parents divorce = I am not worth fighting over. I am not loved because one of my parents is leaving. I cannot trust love. Marriage is not forever." Do this with each life event. Do not breeze through this exercise. Thorough investigation is crucial to bring limiting beliefs to your awareness.

4. Think about what you currently want in life and look for any limiting beliefs you have been carrying around. When we say one thing but create a vastly different result, you can be sure there is a belief at work that conflicts with what you're saying. For example: you want a life partner because that is how you believe you will be happy, but you hold the conflicting belief that you can't trust love. Write down all your conflicting beliefs.

5. Look at each of your beliefs and write down the expectations you formed as a result. Notice that you will have both positive and negative expectations. Using the above example, there is the expectation that being with a life partner would create happiness, and there is the expectation that love may create hurt.

6. Review all the beliefs and expectations you have formed along the way, and look for common themes. You will begin to see a story about your life emerge. Get out your journal and take some time to write down the story you have been telling yourself.

Acknowledge yourself for your honesty in this discovery process. Save all these insights; you are going to return to them later when you get to rewriting your story.

· · · ·

TED'S STORY

I worked in corporate America for ten years, chasing the highest positions and money — and working really hard along the way. It did have its perks, but ultimately, I did not experience the on-top-of-the-world feeling I expected. Although I felt a strong urge to quit, I fought it because I believed I would only find security and an ability to provide for a family of my own in corporate America. When I did my time line, I realized that this belief came from a story I constructed as a teenager when I saw my father lose all our money as a serial entrepreneur. Even though I always felt the entrepreneurial gene in me, I believed working for myself was too risky, which is why I went into corporate America, the "safe zone."

Once I connected these dots, I saw that the story I created in the past about what would keep me from disappointment was actually creating my Expectation Hangover. Finally, I got out! I quit with no job in sight, only faith in myself and a new set of beliefs about what being an entrepreneur could be like. It's now three years later, and I've started my own company. I have never been happier because I'm adding value to the world by living my passion under my rules. I learned that identifying beliefs that were no longer serving me and writing a new story about my life would take me to that on-top-of-the-world feeling I was searching for.

"If you don't change your beliefs, your life will be like this forever.
Is that good news?"
— W. Somerset Maugham

ROLE-PLAYING Rx: THE HORSEBACK RIDER

As much as we want to change our thoughts during an Expectation Hangover, sometimes it feels as though we just cannot get a grip. This is why we need the role-playing prescription of the Horseback Rider. Imagine a horse running free in a field. It would certainly be challenging to catch and contain it! But a galloping horse is steerable and stoppable when a person is riding it. The rider holds the reins, which the horse will learn to respond to. Our mind is similar to a galloping horse in that it seems to run away with us during an Expectation Hangover. We forget that we have thoughts but are not our thoughts. The job of the Horseback Rider is to "ride the mind," observing its pacing and direction, reining it in and redirecting it when necessary. This role helps us achieve greater mastery over our thoughts. Knowing that we hold the reins to our mind and learning to have greater dominion over our thoughts are key to treating our hangover on the mental level.

Throughout this chapter, I am going to be sharing several concepts and tools that stop, or shift the direction of, your thoughts. I invite you to visualize the Horseback Rider — see the reins slowing down or guiding your thoughts — so you become more and more aware of the power you have to alter your response to your thoughts and literally change your brain. Changing how and what you think will become easier as you practice using the Horseback Rider technique and the tools that go with it.

"I feel like I have lost my sense of self, and I am desperate to figure out how I fit into the world after this unexpected turn of events. My mind races through thoughts faster than I can follow, and they often keep me awake all night. I am confused, uncertain, and easily distracted. I have a hard time concentrating on work because my mind seems so out of control!"
— Heath

⟡ **TOOL**
    Whoaing

Your mind needs to be surprised a little with some new sounds because during an Expectation Hangover, it usually sounds like a broken record of the same fear-based thoughts. All of us recognize the sound "whoa" and understand that it means to slow down and come to a stop. In my research with clients, people find this sound calming as well. Just as you would say "Whoa!" to a horse to get it to slow down or stop when it is off and running in the wrong direction, practice saying it to yourself. Try it now: just say it to yourself and see what you experience. Can you feel it bring you more fully into the present moment, where all peace resides? When you notice your thoughts are like a horse galloping wildly in a bad direction, rein them in!

Anne always considered her younger sister her "true soul mate." After Anne supported her sister through a rocky, abusive marriage and divorce, she felt certain that her sister would be supportive of her as she started a new business. Yet she found her sister to be cold and distant, which created an Expectation Hangover. Anne says, "My mind was ruminating, thinking the same hurtful thoughts over and over again; analyzing; finding new ways to explain why she was doing this; being defensive; having inner dialogues with her (where I always won the arguments); and on and on. I knew this kind of thinking was leading me nowhere." She began whoaing whenever she would catch herself thinking hurtful thoughts about her sister. She'd say, "Whoa! Stop, Anne. This is not the direction you want to head." Anne noticed she began to feel more inner peace whenever she used whoaing, because it stopped her from going into a mental downward spiral. Mental rumination does a great deal of harm and only leads to bad moods, depression, and lack of energy.

. . . .

※ **EXERCISE**
Instant Whoaing Technique

Whoaing can be challenging in the midst of an Expectation Hangover, but here is a handy technique you can use to instantaneously whoa your fierce inner critic. Find a picture of yourself as a baby or small child, and carry it with you or put a photo of it on your phone. If you don't have a picture of yourself as a child, you can use any picture of a baby that evokes a feeling of love, as a representative of the little one inside you. Whenever your inner critic is getting loud, take out the picture and look at it. Connect with your original innocence. Know that the person you are being mean to or critical of is that precious child. Look into your own eyes and feel the love that you are. Choose loving yourself over being hard on yourself. You wouldn't be mean to a child, would you? Doing this will immediately shift your energy back into love and help you remember the truth of who you are.

. . . .

Rewiring Your Brain

"If you can get more control over what happens between your ears,
you can transform yourself to become happier, stronger, more resilient,
more loving, more able to help yourself and others."
— Rick Hanson

Your mind is incredibly creative. It can come up with some pretty believable stories. The mind is also malleable. With a greater understanding of the brain, it will be easier to use techniques to better control your thoughts and literally rewire your brain.

Let's start with some very basic neuroscience. Repetitive thoughts form what are called neural nets in our brain, which are clusters of chemically connected or functionally associated neurons. What that means is that if you think the same thought or type of thought over and over, it forms an actual physical cluster of neurons in your brain. Over time these neural nets create "grooves" in your brain that your thoughts gravitate toward. For instance, if you repeatedly think, "I'm not good enough," you create a neural net around that limiting pattern of thought. Once the neural net is formed, it becomes habitual to think in the direction of "I'm not good enough." Thus you will tend to see things that occur in your life through the lens of "I'm not good enough." Since repeated patterns of neural activity change neural structure, you can use your mind to change your brain. This is called self-directed neuroplasticity. Bottom line: neurons that fire together, wire together. You can learn to stimulate different parts of your own brain, which will improve your well-being and functioning.

This will make more sense if I give you a metaphor. Visualize a house in the middle of a really overgrown field. See yourself in a truck that is a football field's distance from the house. Your job is to drive the truck to the house. On your first trip it's a bumpy ride, as you have to get through all the weeds, bushes, and rocks. You are holding on to the steering wheel tightly and are highly focused on your destination. Now imagine you take the same route day after day. Over time the wheels create a path in the field, and eventually, the truck will naturally gravitate toward the path you've carved by driving the same route over and over. It would not require much steering or effort at all. But say you wanted to create a different path to the house. The first time you steered the truck off the grooves of the path you already made, it would once again be a bumpy ride. You'd have to steer with focus to get the truck off the easier, well-worn path. But if you took the new route day after day, a new path would form that would eventually feel as natural as the first path you carved.

Your brain is like the field, and your thoughts are like the truck. If you want to change the direction your thoughts naturally gravitate toward, you are going to have to consciously steer them off their natural course and create new neural pathways in your brain. As you mentally rehearse new beliefs, you install more neurological hardware and put new circuits in place — think of it as a better hardware system for your mind!

✧ **TOOL**
Redirecting

"Nurture your mind with great thoughts,
for you will never go any higher than you think."
— Benjamin Disraeli

After reining in runaway thoughts with whoaing, the next step for the Horseback Rider is to redirect them in more positive, life-affirming directions to create new neural nets in the brain. Just as a horseback rider guides the horse to a desired destination, you can practice and learn to navigate your thoughts. Our reality follows our thoughts, so better thoughts create a better reality.

Redirecting is particularly useful when it comes to negative self-talk. During an Expectation Hangover sometimes the only certainty we can find is in the judgments we have of ourselves. We can look back at what we did that got us to the unexpected place we are in and blame ourselves. Although it does not feel great, it does satisfy the mind's need for certainty. We all have an inner critic who says things like "I am not good enough," "It was my fault," "I should be doing more," "I am a failure," "I'm not worthy," "I need to be thinner," and "Everyone else is better than me."

Perhaps you can relate to receiving compliments but only really remember the one terribly hurtful thing someone has said. Our mind latches onto negativity — it is fuel for the inner critic who has bought into the misunderstanding that being harsher to ourselves than anyone else ever could is a form of protection. Would you consider being in a relationship in which the other person is constantly telling you what's wrong with you? Absolutely not! So why tolerate that kind of relationship with yourself?

Or perhaps you think being hard on yourself is an effective way to produce external results because your negative self-talk drives you to get things done. However, using the voice of your inner critic to fuel you is like putting the cheapest gas into a high-performance sports car. The car would still start, but it would not perform optimally; and the cheap gas would wear the engine down over time. Does that mean filling your mind with pep talks will make it perform at its best? Not necessarily.

Attempting to counteract your inner critic's negative self-talk like "I am a huge failure" by going to the other extreme of superpositive talk like "I am a giant success" creates what I call "pendulum thinking." Let's look at an example: If you had a boss who consistently told you what you were doing wrong and then one day began praising you with compliments, would you be skeptical? Probably. However, you'd be more likely to believe your boss if he simply said, "I know you are doing the best you can. I apologize for being hard on you."

Pendulum thinking creates expectations because we think we "should" be able to hear the voice of an inner cheerleader who fills our mind with positive thoughts, which is especially challenging to do during an Expectation Hangover. As you work with your mind more and more, your thoughts will naturally become more positive, but don't expect yourself to go into cheerleader mode immediately. Instead use Horseback Rider Rx to redirect your thoughts to a more neutral place. Create a new pathway in your brain when you notice yourself engaging in negative self-talk, by saying, "Whoa, stop. This is not the direction I want to go." Then redirect your thoughts by telling yourself some simple but powerful truths such as "I did the best I could — and so did everyone else," "I didn't do anything wrong," and "I am enough." Remember, the brain is predisposed to the negative, so grab the reins of your mind tightly and steer your thoughts to these more positive truths.

· · · ·

CHRISTIAN'S STORY

The most effective way I treated my Expectation Hangover about not being where I thought I "should" be was to force myself to have a serious date with my thought life. Before I did this, my interactions with others were impacted by fearful thoughts that they would "find out" that I wasn't really that successful; that I quit my job;

that a relationship of mine ended; that I was a failure. I had based my supposed lack of success and happiness on the opinions of others, constantly comparing myself to them on Facebook. I had to stop myself from using inner language filled with put-downs and criticism, and think of myself as someone who was valuable as a person and not just for what I could put on a résumé. I learned that I have to stop giving myself such a hard time. I looked back at all the time I spent beating myself up about goals I hadn't achieved, and I reframed them. I didn't finish grad school? Whatever! (My ex-boyfriend had pushed me to do it.) I wasn't married before all my friends and cousins? Whatever! (My parents had pushed me into thinking that was important.) I wasn't working my dream career? Whatever! I have a decent job with a health plan, a 401(k), and a salary that allows me to live in a beautiful downtown apartment where I can use my free time for the activities I am really interested in.

My daily practice is to rein in the wandering, self-defeating thoughts. Every time I start to go down the path of "I should have done this, I could have done that...," I acknowledge the thought and then put it aside and let it go. I focus on the present, and if I do let my mind embrace the past, I do it with a sense of accomplishment.

Redirecting also involves using the Horseback Rider to reframe your beliefs, thereby changing the context of your Expectation Hangover. During the economic downturn, David was a victim of corporate layoffs. In an instant the security of his full-time job was gone, and all he was left with was an apology, a small severance, and a box full of office supplies. Someone who had always taken great comfort in being a planner, David immediately went into a panic, unsure about what he was going to do next and feeling completely lost. When he was not talking about how bad and unfair things were or blaming himself in some way, he was negatively fantasizing about a future of being out of a job for years, getting behind on his career path, having to take out loans, and lots of hypothetical doomsday scenarios — none of which he could be absolutely sure were true. David's thoughts were making his situation far more unbearable than it actually was.

There is our Expectation Hangover, and then there is the meaning we give to it. We often choose meanings that make us miserable. We suffer because we hold on for dear life to the belief that what we are going through is bad and that if our life were different in some way, it would be so much better. All of us at times fall into the trap of making assumptions. But what is actually true is that believing thoughts that make us feel bad continues to make us feel bad. David has the opportunity to redirect his thoughts about his layoff and alleviate his Expectation Hangover on the mental level. Instead of thinking of it as a horrible thing, he can think of it as an opportunity to pursue something new that he never would have done otherwise.

When a client comes to me with an Expectation Hangover, I compassionately listen to their story but do *not* react with the pity or shock they may receive from others or expect from me. I also do not affirm their story by agreeing with how terrible it is that they are experiencing this Expectation Hangover. My intention is to support them in using the tools of whoaing and redirecting, by challenging their thinking.

Sarah was thirty-five and suffering from an Expectation Hangover after her divorce. "If someone had told me that three years after I ended my marriage, I'd still be single, I would have never gotten a divorce." Sarah unequivocally believed her life would be better if only she were in a committed romantic relationship, and she feared she was running out of time to have a family. I questioned Sarah on the assumptions she was making: "How do you know that your life would be so much better if you had a partner? How do you know being single cannot be enjoyable?" After considering the questions, Sarah replied, "Well, actually, I don't know that any of that is true."

Sarah began to realize that what was tormenting her were her repetitive thoughts and assumptions, not the reality of her situation. You will have the same realization when you ask yourself questions that challenge the beliefs that perpetuate your suffering. It is possible to alleviate the mental distress you are experiencing if you remain curious and willing to explore possibilities beyond your old beliefs.

Ask yourself whether there is another way you could look at your situation that is believable and makes you feel better. For example, Sarah began to believe that an amazing partner was in her future but was just taking the time to learn what he needed in order to be ready for her. She also began believing that this time could be a wonderful opportunity to develop a better relationship with herself and have some fun. These beliefs relieved Sarah from being so consumed by all her negative thoughts and freed space in her mind so she could feel peaceful and excited about her present and future.

Even if the circumstances of your life are different, you are no different than Sarah in terms of your ability to overcome your Expectation Hangover by questioning your beliefs and redirecting your thoughts toward new ones. The beliefs you want to be *especially* mindful of questioning are the ones with absolutes like "This always happens to me" or "Things never work out the way I hoped." Beliefs like these imply a sense of permanence to your Expectation Hangover. Bust them by questioning them! How do you know anything will always happen or never work out? The reality is you do not.

I love using Horseback Rider Rx to bust beliefs because it sets us free from unnecessary mental torture. When you ask a new question, your frontal lobe begins to disengage the neural circuits that are connected to old stories that perpetuate your Expectation Hangover, unwiring that old pattern. When your brain isn't firing in the same way, you're no longer creating the same mind.

> "My Expectation Hangover taught me how much our perspective shapes our reality. I saw how rapidly my life changed when I changed my perspective from 'this is the worst thing to happen to me' to 'this is the best thing.'"
>
> — Greg

ASHLEY'S STORY

About a year and a half ago, I officially opened the doors of my holistic health counseling business. I had very high expectations: I was going to be able to quit my day job in a year and go full-time with my counseling. I was going to be a desired health professional in my community, and people would be knocking down my door, wanting to work with me. Well that's not exactly how things are turning out. I had to pick up an extra day at my crap job; I only have four clients; and I am still working my butt off day in and day out to get my name out there. I've dealt with a lot of disappointment and judgment toward myself because I held myself to an unrealistic expectation. I shamed myself for not being the successful businesswoman that I had initially planned to be.

My self-judgment and fear of failure consumed me for a long time — until I got an email from a former client. She wrote how much she appreciated the things I had helped her achieve in her life. Apparently, my encouragement, education, and support had worked, and I had helped one person! It was a huge wake-up call, and I was determined to redirect how I was thinking about my work. I began by believing that it was okay if I did not help thousands; if I could help just one more, it'd be worth it. I learned how to manage my negative self-talk and redirect my thoughts so they were supportive. I began to consider that perhaps I was going through these disappointments so that I could be better equipped to support other women who were going through similar struggles with self-confidence. Recently, I got invited to speak in front of one hundred young girls about building confidence, having self-compassion, and forging a strong sense of self. I know I wouldn't have been able to do this if I hadn't experienced my Expectation Hangover and altered my perspective.

EXERCISE
Rewriting Your Story

You are aware that the story you have believed about your Expectation Hangover most likely is not entirely true. So are you ready to write a new one? You can use the following exercise to challenge your old story and redirect your thoughts to a new one. As you go through this exercise, write your response to each question in your journal.

1. Find a quiet, comfortable place to sit where you won't be interrupted. Go back to what you wrote for Your Storyboard (p. 72) and review the story you have been carrying around.
2. Go back to your Expectation Hangover Assessment Form (p. 28) and review your answers to questions 7–9 (about the beliefs triggered by your Expectation Hangover).
3. Identify and list the similarities between the story you've been carrying around and the beliefs triggered by your Expectation Hangover.
4. For each item in your list, ask yourself, "Do I know 100 percent that this belief is true?" Each time you answer no, run through steps 5–7 in this exercise in regard to the belief.
5. Use the Horseback Rider technique to guide your thoughts from assuming you know the truth to being inquisitive about what else could be true. What new belief (or set of beliefs) could you have that creates a sense of peace, relief, or even excitement?
6. If you believed this new belief (or set of beliefs), how would that affect your experience right now?

7. Start writing your *new* story by completing this sentence: "Instead of thinking the way I have been, I am now willing to think..."

Notice that through the process of redirecting, you are already feeling a sense of relief. You are elevating your consciousness by shifting the vibration of your thoughts. Continue to use Horseback Rider Rx to rein in and redirect your thoughts toward your reframed perspective!

. . . .

"I would never die for my beliefs because I might be wrong."
— Bertrand Russell

THOUGHT TIME TRAVEL

When we're experiencing an Expectation Hangover, the comfort of the present moment escapes us. Instead, we spend a lot of mental energy in the past (which fuels guilt and regret) and the future (which fuels anxiety, worry, and fear). There is a difference between a true *feeling* and a *physiological response* to beliefs or thoughts that create guilt, regret, anxiety, worry, and fear. These states are most effectively treated with the techniques of the Horseback Rider rather than those of the Surfer since they can be alleviated by stopping and redirecting our thinking. Sometimes all the whoaing in the world will not stop your thoughts from time-traveling into the past or future. So I want to offer you some other features of Horseback Rider Rx to steer your mind when it starts to time-travel.

Past-Hacking: Treating Guilt and Regret

Allowing our mind to go to the past to recall fond memories is wonderful. But during an Expectation Hangover, time-traveling to the past is usually not a pleasant trip. I call it "past-hacking" because the definition of *hack* is "to cut or shape with rough or heavy blows." Since when we go back into the past, we are usually either beating ourselves up or living in a fantasy about how much better things were, "hacking" is the perfect thing to call it.

Regret is one of the most common and painful mental activities that we engage in during an Expectation Hangover. We replay scenarios over and over in our head, thinking of all the things we could have done or said, which is miserable. Let me break it down: Something happens. You react, you make a choice, and you take action. Then time passes. And you think about what happened. You analyze it, obsess over it, and talk about it ad nauseam with your friends. You continue to gather information and knowledge. Then you take all this awareness and information you have in your head *now* and beat yourself up because you did not know it *then* — this is both unfair and unreasonable! Regret's cousin is guilt. We experience guilt only when we believe we did something wrong or made a huge mistake. Regret and guilt keep you in the past. When you are consistently looking behind you, it is more difficult to move forward. Think of it this way: If you drove your car by only looking in the rearview mirror, would you ever get to your destination?

Letting go of regret and guilt is possible when we learn from our past and take those lessons into our present and future. We can leverage our past by committing to responding differently in the future. We all make so-called mistakes. Remember, you are human, so stop placing an expectation on yourself that you are supposed to get it "right" all the time! Rewinding time is not possible, and what happened is over. Beating yourself up, wishing it was different, or feeling guilty is not going to change it and is a waste of your precious energy. Next time a similar situation comes along, you will have new awareness and an opportunity to do a little better. Continue using Horseback Rider Rx to guide your thoughts back to this truth: you did the best you could with what you knew at the time.

MAY'S STORY

My best friend stopped speaking to me and ended our friendship because he felt I had let him down and betrayed him. I find it extremely hard to accept what's happened, forgive myself, and move on, because I feel responsible and to blame for everything. He confided in me, and I broke his trust by sharing his secret with another person. I feel awful about it and never thought the secret would get out. As much as I'd like to change the past, I realize that I cannot. I wrote him several apology letters to gain a sense of closure and completion. My disappointment and regret taught me how toxic gossip is in relationships. I am taking this lesson about integrity into my friendships now and have vowed to no longer engage in gossip.

This experience has also made me realize how important trust is in any relationship. I will consider the consequences of my actions and bring my awareness to being a more compassionate and trustworthy person so the love I feel on the inside ultimately shows on the outside.

> "We cannot change the past, but we can change our attitude toward it.
> Uproot guilt and plant forgiveness. Tear out arrogance and seed humility.
> Exchange love for hate — thereby making the present comfortable
> and the future promising."
> — Maya Angelou

 EXERCISE
Releasing Guilt and Regret

Guilt and regret are occupying valuable real estate in your mind that could be used to build upon thoughts that move you forward rather than backward. Using the Horseback Rider to steer your thoughts toward investigation and prevention, this sacred process will help your mind let go of the past rather than rehashing it in your mind. Follow the steps below and answer each question in your journal.

1. Find a quiet, comfortable place to sit where you won't be interrupted. Bring to mind the experience related to your Expectation Hangover that you feel guilty and/or regretful about. When you feel connected to that place, you are going to write a confession. Don't worry — you are only confessing to yourself at this point. (If you feel it would be in service to treating your Expectation Hangover, you may share your confession.) The process of confession is one of unburdening. Include all the details, your reasons, your thoughts, your beliefs about the experience, and so on. Get your guilt and regret over your Expectation Hangover out of your head and onto paper.

2. Attune to your Higher Self and bring forward compassion and understanding toward yourself. Steer your thoughts toward investigation and away from self-judgment, and answer these questions:

What did you learn about yourself?

What did you learn about someone else or a situation?

How would you like to behave differently in the future?

3. Based on what you learned, what commitment would you like to make to yourself about how you will respond in the future? Avoid using absolutes like *always* and *never*, as those words are highly charged with expectation. Instead, consider what kind of agreement with yourself would feel encouraging but not punishing. Here are some examples clients of mine have written as they worked with releasing guilt and regret from their Expectation Hangovers:

> I vow to tell the truth even if it feels scary for me.
>
> I agree to speak up rather than hold something inside.
>
> I promise myself to only pursue romantic relationships with available people.
>
> I vow to listen to my intuition.
>
> I agree to be kind to my coworkers.
>
> I promise to show up fully in my relationships with family members and tell them I love them every day.
>
> I agree to honor the commitments I have made and seek out support to work through the issues that make it difficult for me to keep them.
>
> I vow to be trustworthy by keeping my word with myself and the promises I make to others.

4. Take time to attune to your personal vow, promise, or agreement. You know you are on course when you start to experience some mental relief. Making new commitments assists us in feeling absolved from something that has been keeping us stuck in guilt or regret.

5. Once you settle upon a commitment (you could have several), write it out on a sheet of paper, sign it, and date it. Say it out loud in front of a mirror to truly hold yourself accountable and anchor this sacred process.

Whenever you feel thoughts creep in that lead you back to guilt or regret, use the Horseback Rider technique to guide your thoughts toward your vow instead.

. . . .

Get Your Past off a Pedestal

"The past is a great place and I don't want to erase it or to regret it,
but I don't want to be its prisoner either."
— Mick Jagger

During an Expectation Hangover our mind can play tricks on us like completely altering our memories. We often recall things as much better than they actually were, forgetting the truth and romanticizing our past. This creates senseless suffering.

Glen left his job as a corporate executive at forty-seven years old to pursue his lifetime passion of teaching. A year into teaching he reported feeling a little depressed and wondered if he had made the right choice as he faced dealing with difficult students and a much different salary. He kept thinking about the VIP privileges, recognition, and money that came with his previous job. Once Glen removed the rose-colored glasses he was using to view his past and reminded himself of the pit he had felt in his stomach each day that no amount of money ever filled, his depression lifted. He began to shift his awareness into the truth that he loved teaching and was far more fulfilled than he had ever been at his corporate job, which freed up more mental space to create effective ways to motivate challenging students.

Another extremely common example of past-hacking occurs during breakups. I am astonished at how common it is for people to completely forget how miserable they were in a relationship once it's over. Perpetual thoughts about how great things *were* keep us from thinking about how much better things *are and can be*.

"I had to stop sacrificing my current happiness for an idealized past. The dream of 'what could have been' made me blind to what could be. I learned that the past is no place to linger. The present has to be dealt with and recognized as the foundation to building a successful, fulfilling future."

—Thomas

Stop romanticizing what was — tell yourself the whole truth about your past, not just the things you miss or liked. You can let go of the person or situation and, in the future, re-create the beautiful experiences you had. Write out a detailed and accurate assessment of what you did not like or what was not a fit regarding whatever situation or relationship came to an end. Use Horseback Rider Rx to guide your awareness out of your right brain, where we create fantasies, and into your left brain, where you can get a helpful reality check.

TRANSFORMATIONAL TRUTH
Expiration Dates

Having the expectation of forever — be it a lifetime on a career path, a special someone to share life with until "death do us part," or anything else we believe will have no end — puts us at risk of judging ourselves as failing if something ends. Some relationships, jobs, and situations come with expiration dates, and when we reach them, it is time to move on. This can be particularly challenging if we expected that something was going to last forever (or a lot longer than it actually did).

Say you bought a carton of yogurt with every intention of eating it. It was the flavor you desired, and it satisfied a craving. You scooped out some for breakfast every once in a while, but it reached its expiration date before you finished the entire carton. Now, you could just leave it in your refrigerator. It wouldn't really do any damage, but would you want to eat it? No! The window of opportunity would have passed, and it would be time to buy a new yogurt or move on to having oatmeal for breakfast.

My marriage, something I vowed would last forever, had an expiration date. In our six years together, it was very clear that we were supposed to be with each other — but not forever. Shortly after our wedding, we both faced huge Expectation Hangovers that had nothing to do with each other. My husband was 100 percent the best person to support me during that time, and I was 100 percent the best person to support him. We both were launching our careers as entrepreneurs, and we were each other's biggest coaches and cheerleaders. But once our personal issues were resolved and our careers were moving forward with great momentum, it felt like we were done. As much as we both tried to make it work, the directions in which we were headed were not aligned. Making the choice to separate was incredibly difficult, but it was also the best thing for both of us.

Kirk was a pastor for fifteen years and loved serving his congregation. He came to see me when he began to feel tremendous guilt over feeling apathetic regarding what he thought would be his lifelong profession. Despite his consistent prayer and efforts to reignite his enthusiasm, it was just not happening. When I offered Kirk the possibility that his current job may have reached an expiration date, he reported feeling relieved yet petrified. This was his life plan — how could it be over? At the same time, he could not deny the inner calling to grow in a different way. When he accepted that his current situation had reached an expiration date, it became clear to Kirk that he no longer wanted to be confined to one community — his call to service felt more expansive. It was time to leave his comfortable and certain role. Kirk had the fulfilling opportunity to mentor a young pastor to take his place and then left the country on an international tour of preaching, volunteering, and uplifting, growth-inspiring experiences. I still receive emails from Kirk in which he shares how grateful he is that he did not stay in a situation just because he thought he should.

Just as we cannot allow our need for certainty to keep us in situations that have reached their expiration date, when something stops feeling right, we can't just chalk it up to an expiration date. Most of us enjoy new stimuli. This can drive us to jump out of situations prematurely when they have become boring and unchallenging. Every relationship and job requires reinvention and dedication. We have to be willing to put in the effort, especially when things get difficult, rather than allowing our desire for variety to lead us to mislabel something as having reached its expiration date.

That said, the expectation of forever creates tunnel vision that can be limiting. Our life curriculum is diverse, and just as we moved from one grade to the next in school, we often move from one relationship, job, or other situation to the next in our lives. You do not have to linger in the unpleasant symptoms of an Expectation Hangover when you know a situation is complete. It may be time to throw away the yogurt.

Future-Tripping: Treating Anxiety, Fear, and Worry

Now let's discuss what to do when your mind takes a trip into the future. Future-tripping reinforces anxiety, fear, and worry. Living in anxiety will only intensify the symptoms of your hangover. Not knowing can be downright terrifying, but worrying about it is not going to help you figure it out. Moving into fear will either paralyze you from moving forward or push you into a place of panic, which is likely to lead to another hangover.

We create the experience of anxiety in our body when we are thinking about something that hasn't yet happened. I am certain you will find that almost anytime you experience anxiety, it is because your mind is anticipating some future event. I caution you from buying into the belief that if you figure out what is next for you, you will cure your Expectation Hangover and the anxiety that comes with it.

If you are seeking certainty, you can find it in the present moment. You can be certain of the now and that there will be another now right after it and another now right after that. Think back to a time when someone was deeply present with you, when they looked in your eyes and you felt there was nowhere else they'd rather be. You know how calming that experience is. Hold that space of powerful presence within yourself. Use the Horseback Rider to whoa your mind back to the present moment. In the now, everything else falls away. In the now, all is well.

The most effective route back to the present moment is to take a deep breath. Nothing brings our awareness back to the here and now better and faster than our breath. Try it now. Take a deep breath and notice your mind settle. From this place of presence, the Horseback Rider can rein and steer your mind in the direction you would like to head.

Meditation is the best way to practice being in the present moment. If you are thinking, "I can't meditate; I've tried, and I cannot stop my thoughts," that is all the more reason to meditate. The purpose of meditation is not to have no thoughts; the purpose is to be mindful of how you respond to your thoughts. Sharon Salzberg, cofounder of Insight Meditation Society, explains, "We say all the time in teaching, 'What comes up is not nearly as important as how you relate to what comes up.' So you might have extensive bouts of thinking exceedingly nasty thoughts, but because you are relating to those thoughts with mindfulness and compassion, that's considered good meditation."

You have meditated before, even if you think you never have. Recall a time in your life when you have had a clear, relaxed focus. Perhaps it was when you were playing golf, gardening, painting, dancing, singing, making love, or building something. You have had moments of meditation, and you can use those as reference points. Meditation is not just some hip thing to do — it is an investment in your overall mental clarity. Try to imagine

"I incorporated meditation into my everyday life and finally shut up for long enough to hear my loving self speak up. I listened and heard encouragement and unconditional love instead of doubt and negative talk. Confusion lessened when I sat down and asked for guidance. The best thing to come out of my Expectation Hangover was the practice of listening to that nicer voice during meditation, which allowed me to find the courage, drive, and willpower to make my biggest dream come true."

— Rita

hearing the sound of the ocean while a jet engine flies over you, or tasting the sweetness of chocolate while your mouth has been numbed, or smelling the delicious aroma of freshly baked cookies in a room full of trash, or seeing a breathtaking sunset through a dirty and broken window. In these cases, your senses would be too overpowered by the distraction to fully experience your hearing, taste, smell, and sight. Similarly, when our mind is overpowered by thinking about our Expectation Hangover, we miss out on the more subtle ways our senses communicate with us. When the sea of the conscious mind is calm and clear, you alleviate mental stress and become more receptive to thoughts and insights that will move you out of your Expectation Hangover.

GUIDED VISUALIZATION
Connecting to the Present Moment

You can download the audio version of this exercise at
www.expectationhangover.com/bonus

The most important thing about meditation is to simply do it and release any expectations about how it should be. This visualization exercise will help you observe your thoughts and take dominion over them. Read all the directions so you understand them, then take yourself through the exercise.

1. Find a quiet, comfortable place to sit where you won't be interrupted.

2. Rest your hands on your lap and close your eyes. Take three deep, slow breaths and bring your full awareness to your breath. Feel yourself in this present moment. Feel your seat on the floor or chair, the clothes on your body, your hands on your lap. Use physical sensation to bring you into the now.

3. Imagine that you have a blank, white movie screen in your mind, on the back of your forehead, that you can view with your mind's eye.

4. Allow your thoughts to flow freely but instead of just thinking them, see them on the movie screen. Project your thoughts onto the screen.

5. Practice simply observing the thoughts. Just let them be, floating across the screen like rolling movie credits.

6. Notice that you have choice over which thoughts you want to engage with, take further, obsess over, or respond to. You may not always feel like you have control over every thought that comes in, but you do have dominion over which ones you choose to latch onto.

7. Continue projecting your thoughts on the screen and practice just letting them appear on the movie screen of your mind.

8. Set the intention not to mentally grasp onto any thought. Loosen your grip on the thoughts that float by — just see them move across your mental screen.

9. Continue bringing your awareness back to your breath and repeat inwardly, "All is well." This is the voice of your Higher Self, who resides in the comforting knowledge that all is truly well in the present moment.

10. When you are ready, slowly open your eyes and bring your awareness back into the room.

Use this process to turn down the volume of the anticipatory thinking that produces anxiety and turn up the volume of your Higher Self, which produces peace. Another suggestion that many of my clients have used is to wear a piece of jewelry, or even a rubber band around your wrist, that you deem your "presence piece." Any time you feel your mind future-tripping to an undesirable destination, touch your presence piece and take a deep breath.

. . . .

Fear is also something we create with our minds. We only feel the true physiological reaction of fear when something unexpectedly scares us and triggers our fight-or-flight response. Most of the fear we experience comes from asking ourselves what-if questions followed by an imagined outcome that is negative. The biggest symptom of Katie's Expectation Hangover from being laid off was fear. Her mind was swarming with what-if questions like "What if I don't get another job?," "What if my money runs out?," "What if no one will hire me because I got laid off?," "What if I can't pay my bills and I have to move back in with my parents?," and so on. I explained to Katie that her fear was all in her head. There was not an actual physical threat to her, but she was going into panic mode, which was triggering a fight-or-flight response.

Your mind does not like unanswered questions. Imagine a three-year-old child tugging on his mom's shirt and saying repeatedly, "Mom! Mom! Mom!" in an attempt to get her attention. The more she tries to ignore him, what happens? The tugging gets harder, and the mom-ing gets louder. But as soon as she addresses the child, the tugging and calling out stop. And usually, all the child wanted in the first place was attention and acknowledgment. This is what your what-ifs need when they are galloping away with your mind during an Expectation Hangover: to be acknowledged, addressed, and redirected.

> "Asking a question is the simplest way of focusing thinking....
> Asking the right question may be the most important part of thinking."
> — Edward de Bono

※ EXERCISE
Answering Your What-Ifs

When you notice your mind swirling with a lot of worrisome what-if questions that are creating the experience of fear, use this exercise to rein your thoughts in a direction that calms your mind.

1. Find a quiet, comfortable place to sit where you won't be interrupted.
2. Get out your journal and allow your mind to bring forward all the what-ifs in your head until you begin to experience fear. Write out all the what-ifs that come to mind.
3. For each what-if, write out everything you are afraid might happen — even go to worst-case scenarios because sometimes the mind simply needs to acknowledge the biggest fear you are facing.
4. Use the Horseback Rider technique to whoa your mind and redirect

your what-ifs away from something you are scared of and toward something that feels neutral or encouraging. Here are some examples of redirected what-if statements (taken from my work with Katie):

> What if I get a job I like better in three months?
>
> What if I can use the money from my layoff and actually take a month off, which I really need?
>
> What if getting laid off from this job opens up new opportunities for me?
>
> What if the time away from the stress helps me finally address my thyroid problem?

Can you see how much more empowering these redirected what-if questions are?

5. Each time you feel fear tugging on you, acknowledge that your mind is looping through what-if statements and generating worst-case scenarios. When you notice this, immediately whoa, rein in, and redirect.

"What if . . . ?" is a question that evokes a feeling of wonderful possibility or dreadful panic. Choose possibility over panic!

· · · ·

MELLESSIA'S STORY

I suffered a massive stroke one month after my thirtieth birthday. I was a healthy, active, vivacious woman. Literally overnight, I lost many physical abilities, including standing and walking, along with my career, boyfriend, friends, apartment, smile (my dimples disappeared on the left side), and confidence. It felt as if my independence and optimism had been taken away. I had to move back home to Indiana to be cared for by family, which was humiliating (losing the ability to bathe yourself does that). I went through a phase of depression, refusing any medications, believing I could beat this thing that had taken over my life.

I withdrew into myself to dig deep, and many friends and family members could not understand. Mentally, I was in the war of my life and was not going to surrender. The reintroduction to the world after being in a hospital and rehab facility was the most difficult test of my confidence and sense of self. As a young woman with an "invisible injury," I got a lot of strange looks and comments. Overcoming the negative thoughts about my future was very difficult. All the what-ifs and unanswered questions consumed me. What if I can't ever walk and shower on my own? What if I am unable to return to work? What if I am not able to have children? Will a man ever love me with these deficits? Will I be able to braid my future daughter's hair, the way my mom braided mine? My salvation was to focus on one day at a time to get through those thoughts and say to myself, "What if God has put me on a new course in life for a really good reason?" That question brought me peace.

"I have learned to see the world through my heart, not my mind, because my mind can be like going behind enemy lines sometimes. My heart holds the truth."

— Gretchen

I reframed how I was thinking of my stroke by choosing to believe that my life had been paused for a reason. Today, five years later, I am so full of gratitude for the stroke I survived. I have learned to embrace the change it brought into my life. I keep a perspective of positive vision for my future and hope for all survivors by encouraging others, via social media primarily. I have come to see the stroke as fierce grace. A miracle has occurred in my life because I changed my entire perspective.

The valley was so painful, but the other side has proved to be more than I ever imagined for myself. Ironically, I feel much more beautiful and confident now, in my thirties and poststroke, than I ever did while fighting with myself in my mind during my twenties. I have finally let go of those painful expectations I had. Before my Expectation Hangover, I was rigid and never thought there was any other way. Today I understand the concept of "come what may." I don't worry so much about having a defined purpose or path because all the little detours have provided me so much scenery. Perspective is everything; changing my mind has literally changed my life!

We tend to worry a lot about our future during an Expectation Hangover, as it gives us a false sense of control. When faced with the unknown, worrying is the default habit we slip into because it gives us a way to seemingly deal with our concerns. But worrying is a *huge* drain of your energy and completely useless. I used to be quite the worrywart. When I was a little girl and my parents went out for date night, they'd have to call home once every hour to assure me they were okay because I was so worried something would happen to them. I continued to experience lots of worry into my adulthood until I learned ways to manage it and accept the unknown in my life.

Worry is a by-product of using your imagination poorly. If you are going to future-trip, go to a desirable destination! You're making it up anyway, so make it something that you would actually want. You have so much creative mental energy. Use Horseback Rider Rx to redirect your imagination in a way that creates the feelings and experiences you desire rather than dread. Worry is fear, not love. Your imagination is too creative and expansive to waste on worry. The people in your life are too precious to worry about — send them loving energy and positive thoughts instead. Your time is too precious to waste on fear-based thoughts.

Consider how your Expectation Hangover would be different if you *stopped worrying about the things you can't control and only focused on the things you can — like your thoughts.*

 EXERCISE
Future Forecasting

Are you ready to use your imagination in a way that excites rather than worries you? In the midst of an Expectation Hangover, wouldn't it be nice to have something to look forward to? Well, you do — it is your future, and you get to create it! If you cannot see it clearly, this exercise will help, and it's great fun because you get to dream big.

You are going to write out a vision for your life over the course of the next year. A written vision is different from, and even more creative than, a vision you create with pictures, because writing it, and rereading it regularly, gives you the opportunity to be specific and talk about the feelings you are experiencing. In this vision include all aspects of your life — work, relationships, health and well-being, finances, spirituality, hobbies, environment, experiences, and so on. Consider what you want to be doing, feeling, experiencing, and creating. Include who you want to be with and where you want to be. Get highly detailed, specific, and descriptive. Write out in *present tense* what your life is like as if it is actually happening right now. Stretch yourself and allow yourself to dream big, but make everything in your life vision at least 90 percent believable so you actually buy into it.

To inspire you, here is a snippet from a life vision that a client of mine created for herself after being diagnosed with an autoimmune disorder:

> I am waking up every day feeling rested and vital after a nice, peaceful sleep in my luxurious king-size bed. I turn over and snuggle with my incredible partner, who tells me he loves me every morning. I hear the sound of birds chirping outside and gently get out of bed to open the blinds to my beautiful view of nature. I sit down in my comfy purple chair, light a white candle, and engage in my morning meditation, which I love! My mind calms down, and I am easily able to observe my thoughts and bring my awareness to my breath. After my meditation, I enjoy my delicious tea and do my morning stretches and exercises. My body feels awake and vital. Each day I am getting stronger and healthier as I support my well-being by enjoying delicious, organic food.

At the end of your life vision, write the phrase "This or something better, for the Highest Good of all concerned" so you can be free of any expectations. You only set yourself up for an Expectation Hangover if you expect these things to happen — this is a vision, not a demand. It is wonderful to stretch your mind and entertain the possibility that you could dream a different reality into being. Hold your ideal vision at heart, but hold it loosely. Use it as a destination that the Horseback Rider can guide your mind to whenever you notice worry emerging.

· · · ·

CONCLUSION

If you want to change your life, you *must* change your thoughts. And do so with loving discipline. Remember, your thoughts about what is happening in your life have a far greater impact on your well-being than what is actually happening. Acknowledge your Expectation Hangover as the catalyst for learning how to rewrite your story and reprogram your brain. You do not have to tell yourself an old story that perpetuates your hangover. You do not have to believe all those terrible and limiting beliefs. Your brain is completely equipped to free you from mental suffering.

With the tools you have learned in this chapter, you mind will no longer be a runaway stallion pulling you in undesirable directions. You are the Horseback Rider — you hold the reins of your mind and can stop, alter, and redirect your thoughts. You can see now how your past has brought you into the present and how the present catapults you into the future. Courage is not the absence of fear; courage is feeling fear and moving forward anyway. It comes from the Latin word *cor*, which means "heart." With courage you will go deep into your heart, which is the center of your compassion, and move forward even when you are afraid. Think kind, truthful thoughts. Choose only to buy into beliefs that move you away from your Expectation Hangover and toward the unexpected possibilities that are emerging all around you. Be courageous.

> "What we are today comes from our thoughts of yesterday,
> and our present thoughts build our life of tomorrow:
> Our life is the creation of our mind."
> — Buddha

Chapter Eight

THE BEHAVIORAL LEVEL

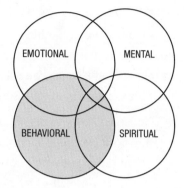

"If you don't go after what you want, you'll never have it. If you don't ask, the answer is always no. If you don't step forward, you're always in the same place."

— Nora Roberts

Are you at the point where you have more inner clarity about yourself but the outside is still murky? Or perhaps you are aware of the actions you "should" take to alleviate your Expectation Hangover but just don't seem to be taking them. The more we analyze our Expectation Hangover, the more we feel that we have a grasp on our reality. But if we linger in the comfort of processing and awareness too long, we move into paralysis by analysis, and things remain the same. Change in your physical reality does not automatically occur once you have an "aha moment" about something — if only it were that simple.

Insanity is defined as doing the same thing over and over and expecting a different result. Ever feel insane? (We all have; you're not crazy!) The behavioral level is where the rubber meets the road in terms of treating your Expectation Hangovers and stopping the insanity. Clients have come to me after years of counseling and therapy and can explain themselves better than any psychiatrist could. They have felt their feelings and can clearly articulate limiting beliefs, yet they still engage in behaviors that are unhealthy or unloving and do not create the results they desire.

You have to leverage your awareness about your Expectation Hangover by actually *doing* something that is inspired by your insight. Awareness without action is merely psychological entertainment. Nothing materializes out of thin air just because we expect to have it. In this chapter we are going to treat Expectation Hangovers by exploring behavior from two perspectives:

- What actions you are taking in relation to your overall well-being and how you can improve the choices you are making.
- What is driving your choices and how you can reorient the way you motivate yourself to take action.

Disappointment can trigger actions that do not always match the desires or dreams we claim to have. We find ourselves either doing nothing at all or doing things that are not creating lasting change. We say we are going to eat better, get our résumé together, hire a coach, or get back in the dating scene, yet find ourselves hovering in the comfort zone of our unmet expectations.

It would seem reasonable to think that not getting what we want would motivate us even more to go after it. Instead, it can be easier to talk ourselves out of doing something than it is to muster up the courage to do it. Why can it be so challenging to change behavior during Expectation Hangovers? During a time when we seriously need some momentum in our lives, how do we get our mojo back?

First, it is important to understand that only about 5 to 10 percent of what most of us do in any given day is driven by our conscious awareness. By "conscious" I mean that we are actively aware of the choices we are making that drive behavior. Unconscious programming drives the other 90 to 95 percent. Visualize an iceberg, which is only about 10 percent above water and 90 percent underwater. Most of our behavior and decisions are driven by what is below the water, what we cannot see. As much as we may believe that we are actively participating in life, the vast majority of what we do is based on habitual behaviors and responses.

Think of what you did this morning. You probably engaged in some kind of routine that you did not really think much about — things like brushing your teeth, showering, making coffee, and driving to work. You were not consciously aware of your behaviors; rather you were simply going through the motions of your life. Just as we create habits involving our day-to-day tasks, we also develop habitual behavior based on the story we've created about our lives and ourselves. All the belief systems you uncovered in chapter 7 influence your behavior even if you are not consciously aware of it.

So how do we bring to the surface what has been unconsciously driving our behavior and not necessarily creating the results we want? That is where some role-playing Rx comes in to help you melt away obstacles. And don't worry — it's not as hard as moving an iceberg!

ROLE-PLAYING Rx: THE SCIENTIST

Before delving into the role of the Scientist, let's get a bit nerdy and examine what a scientist is and does. The word *science* is derived from the Latin *scientia*, meaning "knowledge." (If you haven't noticed by now, I love to understand what words truly mean because they mean so much more to us when we know what they mean. You know what I mean?) *Science* is defined as "a systematic enterprise that builds and organizes knowledge in the form of testable explanations and predictions about the universe." A *scientist* is defined as "a person who studies or practices any of the sciences or who uses scientific methods; a scientific investigator." The scientific method seeks to explain events. A hypothesis is put forward and used to make predictions that are testable by experiment or observation, and then the hypothesis is modified based on the results. A *hypothesis* is "an interpretation of a practical situation or condition taken as the ground for action; a supposition or proposed explanation made on the basis of evidence as a starting point for further investigation."

Using this metaphor, you are the scientist, and the universe you will be studying is that of your behavior. Your scientific method will be to gather knowledge and collect data regarding your actions; observe and investigate the results you have gotten up to now; formulate hypotheses to modify behavior and predict new results; and then apply your hypotheses to treat your Expectation Hangover. Like a scientist, you will observe your behavior without any judgment; investigate what drives your behavior; hypothesize about and test new behavior; and apply proven methods to motivate self-honoring choices. Okay, that may sound complicated. Don't stress out if you're having flashbacks to struggling through high school chemistry — this is going to be much easier and far more satisfying!

Taking on the role of Scientist moves us into becoming the neutral observer and researcher of our own behavior rather than the critic or the unconscious robot. Putting ourselves under a nonjudgmental microscope of awareness, we become conscious of our unconscious, habitual programming. That is how we see the part of the iceberg that has been below the surface, take steps to dissolve it, and get out of our own way. The Scientist is proactive rather than reactive, seeking to find the truth (rather than blame or justification) in every situation. The Scientist is not attached to any specific outcome, but is open and compelled to observe and study your Expectation Hangover. Changing behavior does take practice; but eventually, with the transformational combination of awareness and action, our behaviors match our conscious intentions, and the insanity stops!

"I've learned the deep satisfaction of taking my well-being into my own hands and seeing results come of my efforts, not just in my physical health, but in my overall life."

— Stephen

Self-Care

Your first experiment as the Scientist is to observe and modify the way you take care of your well-being on a physical level. You will put your daily habits and coping strategies under a microscope and examine what needs to be changed. Because an Expectation Hangover isn't life threatening in itself, we often neglect to make major changes to the way we attend to our physical needs. In fact, although our self-care requires closer attention, it is more common to engage in behaviors that are self-sabotaging rather than nurturing.

We add to our suffering by resorting to the behaviors associated with temporary coping strategies — for example, drinking alcohol for a pick-me-up when it actually does the opposite because it is a depressant. Having just a glass of wine or one drink is going to lower the serotonin levels in your brain. Although you may feel better for an hour or two because you've numbed yourself, you will feel even worse the next day because you chemically altered your body in a depleting way. Then we try to pep ourselves up with caffeine; this depletes our adrenal glands, which are already taxed by the stress that comes with an Expectation Hangover. Caffeine is also a stimulant that can affect the quality of your sleep, and you need sleep. Expectation Hangovers can keep us up at night, and when you are not rested, you do not have the mental, emotional, and physical resources you need to treat them effectively.

What you eat not only impacts you in terms of calories and the way you feel, but also in terms of your relationship to your level of self-care. If you are taking the time and consideration to nourish yourself with healthy things like greens, fresh juices, and organic foods, the message you are sending yourself is "I care so much about you that I am only giving you the best." That is much different than the message you send when you consume processed food or sugar or, conversely, when you barely eat. Money is similar to food in that it is a necessary part of life (unlike alcohol, recreational drugs, and caffeine, which we can cut out completely), and during an Expectation Hangover you may go into a behavior pattern of either overspending to try and compensate for a lack you feel or intense financial contraction because your insecurities are triggered. Cultivating healthy financial habits during an Expectation Hangover is nourishing to the part of you that wants to feel safe.

"I was depressed because my dream job wasn't making me happy — it was making me miserable. I overindulged in food and alcohol, and gained weight. I associated drinking with the freedom and carefree experience of college, and thought that by drinking I could bring those feelings back. It was a form of rebellion that was self-destructive and did nothing to alleviate the Expectation Hangover. Relief from my Expectation Hangover began when I stopped taking actions that were repetitive, destructive, and boring. I learned the importance of taking responsibility for my actions and letting go of self-destructive behaviors."

— Lennay

Continuing to neglect our well-being is a problem because it threatens the part of us that is called our "basic self." Our basic self is most concerned with our physical survival needs, like food, sleep, and safety. When our basic self feels unnourished and untended to, it unconsciously triggers primal fears of survival that can show up as increased anxiety, sabotaging behaviors, or even a sense of panic. You can think of the basic self as a young child. When her body is well loved, fed, provided for, and rested, she is an angel. However, if her needs are not being met in some very basic ways, she gets upset and acts out.

This disruption on the level of the basic self leads to common physical symptoms, such as headaches, lack of sleep, weight gain or loss, stomach problems, illness, chronic pain, adrenal burnout, and addictions (to name just a few). Often it's the very symptoms of an Expectation Hangover that make us just uncomfortable enough to make behavioral changes that impact our overall health and, consequently, our life.

Julie was six months into a yearlong commitment at a job she thought she'd love. It turned out the job was nothing like she thought it would be. It was incredibly stressful and crawling with people she did not click with. She would have loved to leave but felt she should stick to her commitment. Julie suffered from headaches and stomach problems. She gained ten pounds; she would have at least one drink at least five nights a week; and she stopped going to the gym. She also slept with her BlackBerry next to her bed and was on it when she first woke up in the morning and, at night, until just before she drifted off to sleep, which was usually restless and brief. Julie justified the drinking by saying she needed stress relief; the eating by saying it was how she rewarded herself; the lack of exercise by saying there was simply no time; and the lack of sleep by saying she had too much work to do. She was scared to ask for a day off and just figured she'd catch up on relaxation at the end of the year. Julie had allowed the Expectation Hangover from her job to trump her physical well-being. And she bought into all her justifications so well that she even forgot how to take care of herself.

Our mind can find all kinds of ways to justify overdoing, undersleeping, overeating, underexercising, and overspending. We think we need the drink to calm ourselves down; deserve the french fries because we've been let down; and can get by on little sleep because we have so much to do. When we step into the role of the Scientist, we examine the negative consequences of our behavior and transition from justifying them to changing them.

When I worked with Julie, the very first thing we did was to create a self-care plan to treat the physical symptoms of her Expectation Hangover immediately. A self-care plan, which you will learn to create for yourself later in this chapter, is a specific list of the behaviors you will modify, stop, or implement in your life. Julie stepped into the role of the Scientist and moved into neutral observation of herself. She then put her lab coat on and created a self-care plan that she hypothesized would treat her very pressing symptoms. Her self-care plan included exercising for at least one hour three days a week; sleeping a minimum of seven hours a night; cutting back to only one cup of coffee per day; turning off her phone at least two hours before bed; and meditating at least five minutes per day. After implementing this plan for only two weeks, Julie immediately began to feel better. Her theories proved true! She had more energy, her headaches and stomachaches went away, and her overall mind-set shifted. As she took care of her basic needs, she actually found her job less stressful. She saw she was using the job as an excuse to not take care of herself (which had also been a pattern in previous jobs). With her clearer state of mind, she became better at communicating with coworkers and setting boundaries with her boss.

KAREN'S STORY

At fifty-seven years old I was permanently disabled after a workplace injury, and my company decided they would not accommodate me. So I found myself unable to work in my profession of thirty years. In one day everything changed. Not what I expected! I had no idea how to plan from one day to the next. Food was my only friend, it seemed, as I sat at home and waited to hear if I had a job. My professional identity was gone. I spent my days, when I wasn't at medical appointments, playing computer games, withdrawing from myself so I didn't have to think about what was happening or how bad I felt. One day I got a glimpse of myself in the mirror sitting in front of the computer with a bag of chips next to me and did not even recognize myself. I saw my so-called coping strategies were only making my hangover worse and realized that even if I did not have control over my job, I did have control over how I coped.

Now I've joined Weight Watchers and begun a water-based exercise program, and I reach out to friends to stop isolating myself. I've also joined a semiprofessional choir, started a writing group, and begun volunteering, all of which help feed my soul in a much healthier (and lower-calorie) way than the food did. My Expectation Hangover taught me that my profession is not who I am. Nor are my medical diagnoses. It is teaching me to listen to my body and my inner voice to learn what they need. I'm learning to love myself, take excellent care of myself, speak my truth, ask for what I need, and be the best me I can be.

Something to be aware of as you observe and investigate your self-care is that we are all prone to addictive behavior, and it comes out the most during an Expectation Hangover. Why? Because we are on the prowl for anything to make us feel better and less uncertain. Addictions are there for us when it feels as if no one else is. Do you know what your addictions are? Some of us have several. Mine has been watching TV, which I do not do on a regular basis. I knew that I was avoiding truly dealing with an Expectation Hangover when I found myself in a pattern of getting totally hooked to a series and spending two or three hours per day watching television. It was my way of zoning out, numbing, and escaping from the reality of my life. Although I temporarily felt better when watching TV, I felt even more hungover the next day, which was an added dose of guilt. Guilt happens when we feel ashamed of our actions, when we know that what we are doing isn't good for us but we do it anyway. When any behavior feels out of balance, admit to yourself that it is addictive.

Addictions of all kinds — to substances, fears, self-doubts, material comforts, work, food, relationships, sex — give us a false sense of freedom. For a moment the high or distraction we get from an addiction feels liberating because it frees us from the symptoms of our Expectation Hangover. However, the freedom we experience from addictive behavior is like a mirage. Compulsive behavior imprisons us because we consistently find ourselves needing it in order to experience what we long for. Only aligning our actions to what truly feeds our body, mind, heart, and spirit offers true liberation.

"I have learned that my coping mechanism is to bury myself in work. I now take Sundays off. Period. I need that day of rest. (God was onto something there.) While one day off a week may not be the typical 'American Dream,' it is just right for me. And I stick to that. I turn down clients and gigs on Sundays. I take a day to rest, regroup, rejuvenate. I am truly a happier, more productive person because of it. I also say no to work that isn't right for me. I don't take a job just to have a job."
— Nicole

Recognize your addictive behavior, but don't beat yourself up for it. When you feel the urge to shop, eat, drink, watch TV, or indulge in whatever your "drug" of choice may be, sit with the feeling instead. Call upon your

Surfer to ride the wave of whatever feeling is coming up and feel it instead of numbing it. Remember that emotion (e-motion) is energy in motion, so get that energy moving in healthy ways. Breathe. Write. Dance. Paint. Meditate. Call a friend or sponsor. If you interrupt a behavior pattern consistently, it will dissolve; but you also have to introduce new, healthy behaviors. You must choose a different action. Even if it's hard. Even if it doesn't feel as good. And even if you don't think you can do it. You can.

Relationships are another important part of self-care. Reaching out for support is an investment in our overall well-being. In chapter 3 we saw that "being strong" is a coping strategy that can be ineffective. Trying to push through everything on your own is exhausting. No awards are given out for being fiercely independent. Asking for help is often the strongest thing you can do. Conversely, there are some boundaries you need to set and hold yourself to when dealing with others. Saying no to someone else's expectations of you can be a way of saying yes to yourself. Remember, your job is to take care of yourself, and setting healthy boundaries with others is an act of self-love.

You *can* choose what you put in your body, how you move your body, the degree to which you allow your body to rest and recover, and how you invest your time. You owe this to yourself; and I assure you that loving discipline will not only alleviate the symptoms of your Expectation Hangover, but also help you lay the foundation for a healthy lifestyle.

> "Take care of your body. It's the only place you have to live."
> — Jim Rohn

✳ **EXERCISE**
Self-Care Plan

In this exercise you will use the role-playing Rx of the Scientist to gather data about your current level of self-care and modify your behavior to improve your well-being. You will draw upon both the creative and analytical qualities of the Scientist to create a comprehensive self-care plan for behaviors you need to eliminate, modify, or add.

1. Take a sheet of paper and turn it so it stretches longer horizontally than vertically. Draw three columns and label them "Eliminate," "Modify," and "Add."

2. In the "Eliminate" column write the behaviors you are committing to stopping completely.

3. In the "Modify" column list the behaviors you will modify, and state specifically how you intend to adjust them.

4. In the "Add" column apply some real TLC and prescribe yourself behaviors that will nourish your body, mind, and spirit.

5. Observe and take responsibility for any addictive behaviors before they get worse. Remember to pay special attention to your relationship with yourself as well as your relationships with others. Are there conversations you need to have or boundaries you need to set with specific people? Is there an ex to stop stalking on Facebook?

To get your scientific juices flowing, below are some examples from a client's self-care prescription plan. This client was experiencing depression, laziness, lack of sleep, and loneliness while engaging in coping strategies like overworking, overeating, and turning to alcohol and men for comfort.

ELIMINATE	MODIFY	ADD
Alcohol for at least thirty days	No electronics for at least two hours before bed	Enroll in a twelve-step program
Reality television	Leave work no later than 6:00 PM and do not check email from 7:00 PM to 9:00 AM	Yoga two times per week
Sugar and gluten for at least thirty days	Adhere to a cash-only budget of one hundred dollars per week for non-essential spending	Fresh green juice three times per week
Dating for three months	Make plans with a loving friend at least once a week	Journal at least five minutes per day

. . . .

Listening to Your Body

"You have the power to heal your life, and you need to know that.
We think so often that we are helpless, but we're not."
— Louise Hay

During an Expectation Hangover be aware of messages your body may be sending you. Often the physical symptoms or conditions that arise are the body's way of sounding an alarm, making self-care even more urgent.

SAM'S STORY

I was working at a top magazine in New York. At first, I loved my job because it was a constant adrenaline high. The stories, the people, and the money were so exciting. Plus, being the youngest person at the company was great for my ego! But about a year into the job, I began to get lower-back pain. The pain went from dull to severe pretty quickly. I did everything I could to relieve it, from yoga, to doctors, to getting a different chair, to icing or heating, but the pain kept getting worse and affected my ability to work. Saying no to awesome assignments led to a massive Expectation Hangover. Why was my back hurting so much? I did not expect to be dealing with chronic pain in my twenties during what felt like the height of my career.

It turns out my body was talking to me, and because the pain became too much to bear, I listened. I began writing out a dialogue between me and my back. What I discovered through this process is that my back was alerting me that the pace of my job was out of sync with my own natural rhythm. It was too intense, and I was sitting at a desk way too much. I was so enamored with the glitz and glamour that I had neglected my desire to travel, move, and connect more deeply with people. This information was empowering and infuriating at the same time. I had worked so hard to get where I was — how could I leave? I kept feeling like I was supposed to be somewhere else even though a big part of me did not want to be. But the more I denied the truth, the louder the pain got. So I chose self-care by listening to my body and resigning from my job. A week after I left, I bought a one-way ticket to Southeast Asia and have been here ever since, working for various nonprofits and nurturing my creative passion for photography. My pace is peaceful; I am content. There is absolutely no glitz and glamour here; however, there is also absolutely no back pain.

Our body is a marvelous feedback mechanism and can give us a tremendous amount of guidance during an Expectation Hangover if we are willing to listen. During the height of my Expectation Hangover about my marriage, my hair began falling out so much that I was running to specialists to try to find out how I could get it to stop. Using the journaling technique of dialoguing with the pain or symptom I was experiencing, I began to write questions to my body like "What is the message you are sending?," "What do you need?," and "How can I respond to you in a healing way?" I asked these questions one at a time and allowed my body to respond by tuning in to my own inner knowing.

I learned that my body was attempting make me aware of how the stress over my untreated Expectation Hangover was affecting me physically. The fear of losing my marriage was manifesting in hair loss. Instead of making a choice about whether or not to stay married, I was stuck in my attempt to solve my hair-loss problem. And that was just one of my distractions! I was also depleting myself by continuing to work, work out hard, fill my schedule, and travel, during a time when I really needed to nourish myself and make a choice. My self-care prescription included gentle yoga classes rather than boot camps; journaling at night to honor my feelings rather than zoning out to television to suppress them; eliminating all alcohol; increasing my intake of green juice; and eating organic, cooked food rather than salads so even my digestion could get a bit of a break. I filled my schedule with things that were replenishing, like time with friends and bodywork treatments, instead of networking events and work projects.

Consider what you can learn from the physical symptoms of your Expectation Hangover. The body doesn't lie, and often there is an action we need to take to cure our physical symptoms. What messages is your body sending you? What self-care actions would help eliminate your symptoms rather than just temporarily relieving them?

Tending to very basic physical needs helps us relax so that we are more fully equipped to continue making the shifts our Expectation Hangovers are inviting us to make. Following my self-care plan gave me the strength to face the discontent I was feeling and deal with the reality that my marriage was coming to an end. And when we finally made the choice to end the marriage, the hair loss stopped completely.

> ⟡ **TOOL**
> **Observation Journal**

"Self-observation brings man to the realization of the necessity of self-change. And in observing himself a man notices that self-observation itself brings about certain changes in his inner processes. He begins to understand that self-observation is an instrument of self-change, a means of awakening."
— George Gurdjieff

Have you ever been to a zoo where they have gorillas? People always crowd around to watch them, and usually there are a few scientists observing their behavior — charting and documenting every move. I want you to imagine that there is a gorilla part of you (a really cute gorilla of course) and a scientist part of you. The gorilla part is the part of you that unconsciously moves through your day, prompted by the old programming of your expectations. The scientist part of you is the part that witnesses the behavior of the gorilla.

Before a scientist formulates a hypothesis, he collects data through observation. To document your behavior so you can study it effectively, start an observation journal that you will keep for at least one week. Get a separate notebook for this purpose. As you go through the motions of your day, be aware of the part of you that is behaving (gorilla) and the part of you that is observing your behavior (scientist). To practice this right now, become aware of the part of you that is reading this book. Next, in your mind's eye, bring your awareness about six feet outside and slightly above your body and witness yourself reading this book. Notice this dual awareness of yourself as both the observer and the subject of study.

Throughout the day, and especially before you go to bed, put on your lab coat and document your behavior by writing it down. The purpose of your observation journal is to study your behavior by examining what actions you took and did not take, what choices you made, and how you reacted to situations that arose. Note the word choice, self-talk, repetitive thoughts, and emotional states that go along with certain behaviors. You do not have to write down every little thing, but be reasonably thorough.

Kate thought that becoming the vice president of a movie studio at thirty-one would bring her happiness and make her dad proud. Instead, she found herself with new problems: increased responsibility, stress, and a huge Expectation Hangover about the fact that the big title did not come with the big feeling of happiness or worthiness she'd expected. Her friend called her a "workaholic." At first, Kate denied that label, but she could not deny that something felt true about it; so she decided to investigate. By completing her observation journal, Kate noticed and tracked behavior that was reinforcing her Expectation Hangover. She noticed she talked a lot about how stressed-out she was and the next step instead of just appreciating where she was. Kate also realized she had started to leave behind her feminine virtues to "keep up" with all the men around her. She was living in a horror story of her own creation because of all the pressure she put on herself. Hard-driving self-talk was incessant, and enough was never enough. Kate passed over compliments without ever taking them in. She said no to social invitations and stopped going to the gym to stay at work later or get to the office earlier.

By taking a step back from her behavior and observing it through the lens of the Scientist, she came to a realization she described this way: "I was indeed a workaholic and was consistently making choices that moved me forward in my career at the cost of my well-being and relationships." Once she understood her behavior was the cause of her suffering, she saw she could be the cause of her own happiness by investigating and altering her behavior. (A little later in this chapter, you'll hear about the drastic changes Kate made in her life.)

・ ・ ・ ・

✳ **EXERCISE**
Collecting Data and Formulating Your Hypotheses

Take a week's break from reading this book so you can go into full research mode. Spend seven days as the Scientist and observe your own behavior;

record your observations in your observation journal. When the week is complete, come back to this exercise and respond to the following questions in your regular journal.

1. What am I doing, or not doing, that is making the symptoms of my Expectation Hangover worse?
2. What actions or choices have I been engaging in or making repeatedly while expecting a result different from the one I keep getting?
3. What is my self-talk like?
4. How am I talking about myself and my life with others? What are most of my conversations about?
5. Did I take actions that moved me out of my comfort zone?
6. If I attained a goal or achieved a result, how did it feel?
7. To what degree have I been following my self-care plan?
8. What did I do that was reactive?
9. What did I do that was proactive?

As the Scientist, begin to formulate hypotheses regarding the most appropriate steps to take to alter your behavior and establish healthier, more productive habits, based on the data you collected. Right now you are just investigating. You will not know if change occurs until you test your hypotheses. Use the following prompts to formulate hypotheses about your Expectation Hangover:

> If I stop doing…, then…(Complete as many of these as possible.)
> If I start doing…, then…(Complete as many of these as possible.)
> If I start talking about…rather than…, then…
> My comfort zone is…, and a step I could take out of it is…

Now go out and begin testing your hypotheses to determine what behaviors move you out of your Expectation Hangover. Based on your results, continue to collect data in your observation journal, and formulate updated hypotheses that you then test. This process is not just scientific; it's also empowering! You will see how even the slightest changes in your behavior can create significant positive shifts in your life.

· · · ·

CARL'S STORY

I had been an athlete ever since middle school. I enjoyed it but struggled with fear and performance anxiety. I completely devoted myself to training, hoping I would eventually be good enough to perform even when the anxiety showed up. One day I was competing in a race, and I was in the best shape of my life. I dug deep, moved through the fear, and crossed the finish line with a time faster than I had ever dreamed of. I had always imagined that the moment I finally conquered my demons and performed to my athletic potential would be euphoric.

It was the opposite. A few minutes later, I felt completely deflated. It seemed that no one but me cared. None of my dedication, discipline, and determination seemed to matter at all. I could not help but wonder, what was the point of being an athlete? Somehow I expected my life to be dramatically better now that I was fast, strong, and fearless. But the next day, I woke up, and everything seemed the same.

After crossing the finish line and not seeing the rainbows and fireworks I had expected, I had a very difficult time getting motivated to do anything. Up until that race, I was driven, determined, and disciplined, and in all honesty, addicted. I wanted that fast time so badly, but once I had it, it did not have the huge impact I expected. All my drive was gone. I had lost my mojo. I sat around and could not bring myself to care about anything. I spent a lot of time asking myself questions: Why do athletes do what they do? Why does it matter? How are they being of service? How are they contributing? I could not understand the point of winning at sports or why it mattered, and why I wanted it so badly.

Recognizing that exercise had become an addiction was a huge turning point for me, and in order to quit the addiction, I actually had to allow myself to get out of shape for a period of time. Obsessively exercising was a way for me to avoid dealing with other aspects of my life where I had been struggling. I was also addicted to being in control of how my body looked, and letting this go forced me to take a painful and honest yet necessary look at what was driving me.

I discovered I had been motivated by deeply rooted insecurities and a need to prove myself. I had juicy demons when it came to fear, and I was on a mission to overcome them. I had to find another way to be motivated not only to exercise, but to do anything. I began by seriously reflecting on why I was an athlete in the first place. When I went through a process of digging deep and learning that my drive was all about proving myself, I no longer felt a powerful urge to do it again. Although disappointing, that final push to the finish line physically released more anger than I knew was there.

I have begun reconnecting with my inner athlete — the part of me that played sports because I enjoyed the feeling, not for the result. Knowing that I have that athlete inside of me who I can trust to show up when I need him has empowered me to be with fear and move forward anyway, in all other aspects of my life. I give my inner athlete what he needs — regular opportunities to flex and strengthen his courage muscles; and he gives me what I need — a deep well of courage.

I have worked hard on recognizing that the highs we get from onetime events like sports competitions and vacations are fleeting and only permanently change the fabric of the rest of our lives if we look hard for the lessons.

COMPENSATORY STRATEGIES

"Pain pushes until vision pulls."
— Michael Beckwith

Consider this: what you are good at may not be good for you. Expectations based on what you were successful at and that have driven your behavior may be blocking you from truly knowing and expressing your most authentic gifts, as was the case with Carl. Coming up with new actions to treat an Expectation Hangover without first investigating the expectations that drove the original behavior is like building a house on an unstable foundation full of cracks. You may be able to build something that stands for a while; but eventually, the weak foundation will give way, and the house will collapse. Similarly, putting new behaviors in place without excavating the previous foundation may produce short-term results but will not lead to lasting changes.

By now you understand that we all experience things that are painful. We develop some form of defense mechanism, such as denial, repression, or rationalization, to safeguard against feelings and thoughts that are too difficult to cope with. On top of our defense mechanism, we also develop a compensatory strategy, which takes a defense mechanism one step further. Whenever we feel unworthy, unsafe, unlovable, or broken, our ego develops a strategy to compensate for whatever is missing. We buy into the misunderstanding that being ourselves is no longer enough. This compensatory strategy then informs the choices we make and actions we take, especially during an Expectation Hangover, when our safety and worth feel threatened.

The following formula shows how a compensatory strategy develops and operates in your life:

Painful things happen ⇨ Defense mechanism (protection) ⇨ Compensatory strategy (to compensate for insecurity, lack, or fear) ⇨ Survival ⇨ Result (not fulfillment)

Note that the result in this formula is *not* fulfillment.

Before you step into the role of the Scientist and research your own compensatory strategy, I'll share mine. As a child, I had no expectations of myself and expected the best from others because I did not have evidence to the contrary. As a little girl, I was happy, outgoing, and engaging, and I loved people. Then, in fourth grade, a group of girls formed the "I hate Christine club." I was teased and left out, and I isolated to protect myself. I felt sad, lonely, and ashamed. My expectations regarding how I would be loved and accepted for being myself were shattered. This Expectation Hangover led me to form a story that I was completely unlikable and something was wrong with me.

The compensatory strategy I developed to distract myself from the pain and make up for what I felt was missing was to become obsessed with accomplishment. I became an achievement addict, in an effort to prove my worth. Getting a B on anything was unacceptable to me. I relentlessly pushed myself to some imagined future that I believed would finally give me the external validation I longed for.

And I did it. I had an extremely successful career at a young age because

I was so driven by insecurity. This compensatory strategy was tied to my survival and sense of worthiness, so it was very strong. But I was still miserable because the very thing that was driving me was sitting on top of an old story that was full of pain. I consistently had Expectation Hangovers when I would accomplish something that I thought would make me feel better about myself yet did not.

Understanding why you do what you do leads to lasting change. Our compensatory strategy (or strategies) absolutely informs and influences the choices we make and actions we take in the present, which impact our future. Often it takes an Expectation Hangover to get us to question the behaviors that have gotten us where we are and to motivate us to investigate and transform our actions.

WHITNEY'S STORY

I had my dream job in the big city of Chicago and my dream guy, who seemed like "the one." Then I lost it all. I was informed via text from my boss, "Don't bother coming in tomorrow." I moved home and started working... at my high school job at the small-town movie theater. I was mortified. How do I explain this to all those people from high school? I'm behind the concession stand while they're standing out there with their wives and husbands and children, spending the money they earned at their great jobs — and I'm wearing a faded red bow tie. Then the day my boyfriend was supposed to arrive for Christmas, he calls and says, "I don't love you anymore, I can't be with you, and I've met someone else." I collapsed like an actress in a bad black-and-white movie. Not only had I regressed to my high school job and home, but my future husband (as I looked at him then) had dumped me a few days before Christmas. I didn't know how to go on. For three days I drank through my parents' wine stores in the garage. I didn't leave my room. I didn't want to feel anything. I wanted to evaporate off the face of the planet. I had lost the entire life I had worked so hard for. I jumped on shady free dating sites. Anything to prove that I was a catch.

I figured if I didn't deal with my Expectation Hangover and just had fun, eventually, it would be far enough in the past that it wouldn't matter anymore.

After a brief time playing out this pattern of wine and darkness, my inner self said, "Get up. This is not how to deal with the hardships you're facing." I saw how destructive my behavior was and started to turn around once I had a big realization: I learned that I created my Expectation Hangover. Here's how: During college I got so motivated by the external signs of being success-ful — great job, knowledge, romantic relationships. I wanted to be validated externally. I totally disconnected from my "soft spot," where my soul and the Universe come in to whisper knowledge and where my true desires live.

I was driven by what my ego wanted, not my soft spot. I'd forced things into existence that weren't meant to be. Eventually, the universe will make you listen to your soft spot. And that's just what it did. It pulled the rug out from under me, twice. And I realized I'd better start listening.

I started to journal a lot, to reconnect to who I truly was and what I truly valued. I let my need for external validation go and put my trust in the Uni-verse. And then things started to happen. I have a new job that came from a random conversation with a woman at a cocktail party. I met a man and am not in a codependent relationship, where if one leaves, the other dies (I learned my lesson from my breakup). In just one year, my whole life is on a different track, and it's never been easier. All those years, I was clinging so hard to a dream that was fueled by an insatiable need to be validated. When I finally stopped looking outside myself, gave myself the approval I was seeking, and let go of my ego-constructed dream, I could hear the whispers of my soul.

Stephanie grew up with a mother who was not very involved in her life. Stephanie never felt truly loved or wanted, or like she belonged. The com-pensatory strategy she developed was to be a caretaker because that was the very thing she longed for the most. Her pain over not feeling loved or wanted pushed her to go above and beyond to make others feel loved and give them a sense of belonging. The payoff was that she felt she had a place in the world — taking care of others. Yet she experienced repeated Expectation Hangovers about the disappointment she would feel after going above and beyond for someone else and then feeling that her love was not reciprocated.

Compensatory strategies come with payoffs and costs. The payoffs are the results we are able to create; the undesirable feelings and experiences we are able to avoid; and the comfort we get from behaving in a way that makes us feel accepted, validated, safe, worthy, or loved. The biggest cost of a compensatory strategy is that although we may create an external result, that result often comes with an Expectation Hangover. As an achievement addict, I was consistently stressed-out and focused on the next best thing to shoot for. I never felt I could relax. For Stephanie the cost was that being such a caretaker eventually built up resentment because she was not getting anything back. We become so consumed with the pursuit of our compensatory strategy that we never stop to ask, "Who am I, and what do I really want?"

Rudi grew up in a household with very strict parents, and he longed to be acknowledged and feel his parents approved of him. In order to get that desired approval, he became a doctor; both his parents were doctors and expected him to be one as well. When he came to see me at thirty-one years old, he was suffering from a debilitating Expectation Hangover regarding his profession. Being a doctor was never his dream; it was his parents' dream for him. Because he was so driven by his compensatory strategy of seeking validation, he never explored what inspired him, and ended up working hard for a degree that he never really wanted. Whenever your choices and actions are fueled mostly by a compensatory strategy, the costs will always outweigh the payoffs.

To help you uncover your own compensatory strategy, this section outlines some common compensatory strategies and explains how they develop. You may identify with more than one of them, as some characteristics overlap; however, there will be one that stands out as the motivation that drives your choices and behavior the most. As you review these, also consider the behaviors your primary caregivers modeled — especially anyone you looked up to or whose approval you sought. Many times we learn our compensatory strategies from others: we either decide to be just like them, or we choose a completely opposite strategy.

High achiever. If you use this strategy, you are highly driven and have
    accomplished a lot in your life. You feel best about yourself when
    you achieve. You have been acknowledged for your accomplish-
    ments and are perceived as successful. Failure is not an option, and if
    you judge yourself as failing in any way, you are unreasonably hard

on yourself. The next milestone is always on your radar. You developed this strategy to make up for feeling you were not enough just being who you are (based on criticism, teasing, or feeling left out). Or you could have developed this strategy because you were only rewarded for your accomplishments (and the reward felt like love).

People pleaser or chameleon. When this is your strategy, making sure everyone else is happy and likes you is a priority. You put others first and do whatever it takes to avoid upsetting someone else. You avoid confrontation at all costs. Pleasing others and having them like you makes you feel safe and loved. You have an uncanny ability to read the people in a room and morph into whatever it takes to make them feel at ease. You thrive on being whoever you need to be in order to blend in and avoid any negativity. You tend to be outwardly optimistic and can act like everything is fine even if it isn't. Perhaps you grew up in a house where there was a lot of fighting and upset, or strong personalities, so you became a peacemaker or highly adaptable. You may have developed the people-pleasing/chameleon strategy to avoid getting picked on. Or maybe you were acknowledged early on for being a "good girl" or "good boy" and thought putting your own needs aside was the way to get love.

Type A or control freak. With this strategy, you get a lot done and love to be in control. You are a great planner, think everything through, and feel best when things are going your way. You'd rather take something on yourself than delegate it. "Going with the flow" is completely ineffective for you. This strategy often develops when your trust was violated in some way and you decided the only person you could rely on was yourself. It can also develop as a result of a rattling Expectation Hangover that happened at a young age, causing you to believe that controlling things was the way to manage and prevent the unexpected.

Validation and approval seeker. This strategy makes you overly reliant on feedback from outside sources. You desire to be seen, heard, and liked. This develops from either an overdeveloped or underdeveloped ego: either your parents always made you feel you were the best, so your sense of worth was constantly dependent on outside validation; or you never truly felt seen or supported by any healthy parental figure, so you were on a constant quest for outside approval to make up for it.

Performer or comedian. If your strategy is to be a performer or comedian, everyone loves being around you because you prefer to keep things light. Going deep or being in uncomfortable situations is torture. You prefer to make people laugh, to entertain them. You might be sarcastic or eccentric, to divert people's attention from seeing who you truly are. These strategies develop because you found distraction was a useful way to keep yourself safe and fit in somehow. You might have grown up in a chaotic household where you became a performer to distract people from engaging in the chaos. Perhaps you use humor as a way of avoiding vulnerability because you feel insecure or unable to express your deep feelings. Sarcasm can be a sneaky way to bring out hidden anger or aggression. Or you may have had big feelings as a child but did not feel safe to express them, so distracting yourself and others became a strategy for channeling that energy.

Rescuer or caretaker. If your strategy of choice is to assume the role of rescuer/caretaker, you take care of everyone else. You are the person people call when they need something, because you'll drop everything to help them. Boundaries are a challenge for you. You often find yourself in relationships with needy people and spend more time attempting to rescue them than caring for yourself. You want to make sure everyone feels they belong and are extremely sensitive to the needs of others, often at the expense of your own needs. This strategy develops from feeling responsible for making sure someone else was okay (usually a parent) early on. Your sense of worthiness came from being there for someone else, and you avoid your own pain by caring for others.

Perfectionist. If you embrace this strategy, you are unsettled by things that are not absolutely perfect. You give 110 percent to everything you do and worry a lot about doing things "right." You have extremely high standards and rarely feel you are measuring up to them. You don't tolerate mistakes, and you are hard on yourself. You delay doing things, even things you *really* want to do, because you think everything has to be perfect before you can begin. The perfectionist strategy develops from growing up in a very judgmental environment. Often perfectionists grew up with parents or authority figures who were hard on them in the name of love and dished out a lot of "constructive criticism." This criticism was internalized and now fuels the belief that love means pushing yourself hard, which drives the perfectionist behavior.

Busy bee. If your strategy is that of the busy bee, you rarely sit still. There is always something to do, and your entire schedule is full. Most of the time, you feel stressed, possibly overwhelmed, yet you get a high from constantly being on the go. You tend to be a worrywart and experience high levels of anxiety. You take on much more than most people could handle and pride yourself on being busy. This strategy can develop from rarely feeling peace or safety and needing a strategy to distract yourself. It can also come from experiencing a highly traumatic situation and not having the support system or tools to process it, which causes the pain to get lodged inside you. Keeping busy keeps you from having to feel or think about the pain.

Judger. If you've adopted this strategy, you have an opinion about everything and everyone. You are highly skeptical and need things proved to you before you trust. You judge yourself harshly, protecting yourself by being much harder on yourself than anyone else could be. Your expectations are extremely high. You tell yourself that judging is a wise thing to do because it is important to think things through. You talk about things far more frequently than you actually do them, and you tend to err on the pessimistic side. Gossip may be something you find yourself indulging in. This strategy comes from growing up in a very fear-based, expectation-heavy environment where nothing was trusted until it was evaluated. People with very strong opinions and negativity surrounded you.

※ **EXERCISE**
Researching Your Compensatory Strategy

Now that you've read about compensatory strategies, it is time to put yourself under the microscope again. Remember to stay in Scientist mode and come from the neutral place of research so you can gather a clearer, more comprehensive understanding of what drives your behavior. Judging or overanalyzing your compensatory strategy is not necessary. When you feel you are in research mode, move through the following steps, answering each question in your journal.

"My self-worth was wrapped up in being able to make other people feel good. I was always the kid who could make everyone else laugh or was put on the spot to entertain people. I was called the 'funny' one and the 'people person.' I remember, as a little boy, wanting to grow up and have a job where I didn't feel so much pressure to be 'on' all the time. I ended up going into sales because I was always told I had the personality for it; however, I actually hate it. I am learning now that my worth is not rolled up in making other people feel a certain way and I deserve to make myself happy first."
— Adam

1. Identify your primary compensatory strategy. Choose from one listed in this chapter or name your own.

2. Describe the development of your compensatory strategy. What happened to you that made you feel inferior, unsafe, or unworthy? Or what happened that made you feel so loved and rewarded that you decided you must do it all the time to continue to feel that way?

3. Describe the ways your compensatory strategy has driven your behavior. What actions have you engaged in as a result of using this strategy?

4. List the payoffs of your compensatory strategy. What has it helped you accomplish? What positive experiences has it created?

5. List the costs of your compensatory strategy. How has it hindered you? In what ways has it depleted you?

6. How has your compensatory strategy contributed to your Expectation Hangover?

. . . .

YOUR SUPERPOWERS

"We must have the daring to be nothing but ourselves
if we are to know what true power is."
— Danielle LaPorte

You are now entering into the part of your research experiment that is my favorite part, which is discovering the qualities that make you uniquely *you*. "Qualities" are the natural characteristics that make you who you *truly* are, whereas the compensatory strategies we've been discussing were developed so you could be who you *thought* you needed to be.

You were born with these qualities. They were not created from a place of lack or fear. I call these qualities your "superpowers." When you know who you are, you are inspired to act from that place rather than from your compensatory strategies, and that creates superpowerful results!

As you research your superpowers, make the Scientist eccentric, playful, and imaginative, like Emmett "Doc" Brown in *Back to the Future*. This Scientist will go back in time to detect the unique superpowers that will drive future behavior. Begin by bringing to mind something that you absolutely *love* doing. When you do this thing, time stops, and you are fully present. Maybe it is painting, dancing, being with your family, cooking, singing, shopping, being in nature, or writing. You can also ask yourself, "What fascinates me?" This question is very different from "What am I good at?" Here is the key: what is important is *not* the activity, but rather the qualities that come out in you while you are doing it.

"For someone who had been an overachiever his whole life, this idea of love that you didn't have to earn with accolades was very powerful and transformative for me. I drew a line between others' somewhat insane expectations of me and my own expectations of me. And I stepped into things about me I love that were not always acknowledged, like my snarky sense of humor and creativity. I now focus on what I expect of me, which is to put my God-given talents to good use."

— Jimmy

For example, I love facilitating workshops, coaching people, speaking, and writing. When I'm doing those things, I am compassionate, inspired, creative, authentic, playful, giving, present, wise, intuitive, nurturing, and loving. Those are my superpowers, the qualities that make me uniquely who

I am. When I tap into those superpowers and take action based on them, I create superpowerful results in the form of retreats, speeches, courses, books, and so on. It is not my overachieving compensatory strategy that is *driving* me to *produce* those results. Rather it is my superpowers that are *inspiring* me to *create* experiences that are deeply fulfilling. (Even though I've described activities tied to my career, these aren't the only activities I love or that bring out my superpowers. I also *love* being with my nephews, and whenever I am, the same qualities come forward.)

EXERCISE
Claiming Your Superpowers
(and an Extra-Credit Assignment)

Bring to mind several things you love doing or experiences you have had that you have thoroughly enjoyed. You do not have to pick something that is tied to a job. List all the qualities that emerge when you are engaged in something you love. Look for qualities that occur across multiple experiences. Choose five to ten of the most consistent and enlivening qualities and name them your superpowers.

For extra credit: Design a superhero outfit that represents your number one superpower. And then go out in public in your outfit. Now, you may think this is completely silly, but going out in your superhero outfit dissolves your compensatory strategy by giving you the experience of fully stepping into your superpower. I, of course, have one too! My top superpower is intuition because when I am tapped into it, I am also connected to my other top qualities. I have a purple cape with a big eye on the back of it, which represents the third eye. I also cover myself in glitter and sparkles, which makes me feel magical. I carry a wand and grant wishes for others, as helping people is a great joy of mine. If you choose to take on this extra-credit assignment, please post a picture of your costume on my Facebook page (http://tinyurl.com/christinehassler) — I'd love to celebrate and acknowledge your superpowers!

. . . .

Remember Kate, the stressed-out vice president who began observing her behavior after she outed herself as a workaholic? Once she realized that her whole career was motivated by the compensatory strategies of high achieving and approval seeking, she embarked on a soul search to discover her superpowers. Kate was able to see how her inner and outer behaviors were affecting the lack of connection she felt, including a lack of connection with herself: "I had reached a level of success that few of my friends had seen, and so I felt a bit lonely and alienated. I also started to form an unhealthy 'better than / less than' comparison game, which served as a defense mechanism until I realized that it was keeping me separate from what I really wanted, which was connection with others."

The qualities she found within that lit her up were joy, love, creativity, and service. She knew that her big corporate job was not in alignment with her superpowers. So she made the big, scary leap out of the corporate world to pursue her heartfelt calling of being of service to humanity in the form of beginning her own network (Synergy TV). Kate says, "I have learned to overcome an Expectation Hangover by just showing up and doing what I love. I used to sell horror movies, and now I promote inspirational stories while sharing my own path of transformation. I had to see what I wasn't to know what I am."

When you replace your compensatory strategy with your superpowers, it will not only support the actions you take when treating your Expectation Hangover, but also become the very thing that informs your choices on the behavioral level from that point forward. The formula that *inspires* behavior, rather than *driving* it, looks like this:

Superpowers $\Rightarrow$ Inspiration $\Rightarrow$ Result $\Rightarrow$ Fulfillment

Use your superpowers to give yourself the very thing the compensatory strategy has been yearning for. For instance, if it has been seeking approval and validation, give yourself those things by stepping into qualities like self-compassion and acceptance. If you long to be taken care of, amp up your level of self-care by embodying qualities like nurturing and loving. If you thrived on making others happy, make yourself happy first by embracing joy. When you give yourself internally the experience you were looking for externally, you will decrease the symptoms of your Expectation Hangover because you will have no expectations of anyone or anything else.

When you are aware of, and have tapped into, your superpowers, there is nothing to compensate for. And you have your Expectation Hangover to thank for this amazing scientific discovery! Now your assignment as the Scientist is to go into observation mode when it comes to your behavior. Before you make a choice or take an action, investigate whether you are being *driven* by your compensatory strategy or *inspired* by your superpowers.

Being inspired is *much* different than being driven, or even motivated. *Inspire* means "to draw forth or bring out and to exert an animating, enlivening, or exalting influence." It contains the Latin root *spirare*, which means "to breathe," so you can think of being inspired as breathing life into something. Ah...Doesn't that feel so much better than trying to compensate for something?

Take a deep sigh of relief. Your compensatory strategy no longer needs to drive you. It has gotten you this far; thank it and instruct it to sit in the passenger seat so that the skills it brings to the table that are still useful can give direction when you request it. Your superpowers are driving the car now.

TRANSFORMATIONAL TRUTH
You Can Have Anything You Want — but Maybe Not in the Package You Expected

What we are really craving when we want something are the experiences and feelings we presume we will get from what we desire. But often we are so obsessed with the form that we forget what is at the root of our desire and miss out on how we could have the essence of what we want right now.

Perhaps your spouse is consistently disappointing you, and you think that if they would only do the things you expect of them, you would feel more loved. You are likely missing out on all the ways they are demonstrating their love to you, and depriving yourself of feeling loved by them. Or maybe because you are obsessing about needing more money, you do not see all the ways you are already abundant, such as in health, helpful people, and opportunities. Attachment to the rules we make about how things "should" look creates tunnel vision, blind spots, and lots of unnecessary suffering!

Take a moment to look around the room and notice everything that is blue. Really look for all shades of blue and create a mental list of the things you see: maybe the sky through your window, a shade of blue on a pillow, the blue in a painting — wherever the color may be. Now, after you read the next question, it is very important to close your eyes immediately. No cheating! When you're done, open your eyes and come back to reading. Here is the question: Can you list all the things in the room that are green?

Now look around the room and see how much green you did not remember seeing because you were attached to seeing blue. All those blue things you are obsessed with finding or having are making you blue!

Ask yourself what fantasies you have conjured up about what your life is "supposed" to look like. To attract more of what you desire, let go of your attachment to the form by replacing expectations of specific outcomes with the feelings and experiences you long for. For example, if you are miserable in your career, write a list of all the things a future dream job will provide in terms of what you would be experiencing and feeling. These things may include feeling you are using your gifts, a sense of giving back or making a difference, being creative, or working with people you enjoy being around. Instead of being attached to a future job that generates those things, become actively involved in generating them now. Step into your superpowers by going beyond your job description; give back by volunteering; create new projects or hobbies; or join a sport or class where you are part of a team.

Consider what you are not attracting into your life because you are overly attached to the package you'd like it to come in. Don't be shortsighted and stubborn when it comes to the way your happiness is packaged. Be open to being pleasantly surprised!

AVOIDANCE TRAPS

*"Right now you are one choice away from a new beginning —
one that leads you toward becoming the fullest human being you can be."*
— Oprah Winfrey

Now that you have reclaimed your superpowers, you probably feel ready to go out and conquer the world, which is wonderful! But before you throw on your cape, I would be remiss if I did not warn you about a trap you may fall into — the avoidance trap. I have noticed that people spend a lot of time talking about what they want to move toward, but they invest a lot *more* time and energy avoiding what they want to move away from. Any choice we make or action we take is moving us either *toward* something we want or *away from* something we don't want. Whatever Expectation Hangover you are treating now probably is not the first one you have ever had. You have been disappointed before. The more painful the Expectation Hangover was, the stronger the vow you made to avoid feeling like that ever again. Over time this vow has motivated a lot of "away from" actions that have led you to fall right into an avoidance trap.

For example, I experienced a lot of rejection during years of feeling left out and a series of unrequited crushes. Consequently, despite wanting to be "out there" in my personal and professional life, I would do whatever I could to move *away from* rejection. I took fewer risks, kept to myself, rarely flirted, played it safe in my career, and did not pursue friendships because of the fear of being shot down.

Jacob's avoidance trap came from feeling insecure. He grew up in a military family and moved almost every year. Not only did he feel self-conscious every time he had to enter a new school, but he also was never in a home or city long enough to feel secure there. As he got older, moving away from anything that felt insecure or impermanent motivated his actions. He went to college, got a job at a company, and bought a house. Nearly seventeen years later, when he came to see me because of his Expectation Hangover about his life being unfulfilling, he was still living in the same house and had the same job. He felt secure but knew he was not living up to his full potential. Jacob was aware that creativity was his key superpower, and he always dreamed of pursuing his love of music and possibly moving to Nashville; but his fear of insecurity kept him exactly where he was — in an avoidance trap.

Other common reasons for falling into avoidance traps include fear of the following: feeling out of control, uncertainty, abandonment, intimacy, vulnerability, disappointing others, and being judged. None of those things are desirable experiences, and I can appreciate why anyone would want to avoid them. We think we are keeping ourselves safe and avoiding pain, but avoidance traps become just that — traps! They keep us from moving toward the feelings and experiences we actually *do* want, and our superhero costume continues to collect dust in the closet.

 EXERCISE
Escaping Your Avoidance Trap

Think of this process as a rescue ladder out of your avoidance trap. As you move through the following steps, answer each question in your journal and capture any insights that arise.

1. Determine what your particular avoidance trap is. What feeling or situation do you not want to experience? What will you do almost anything to avoid?

2. Identify what you are missing out on when you're avoiding the thing you fear. In other words, what is your avoidance trap preventing you from doing? How is it limiting you? What is the cost of your trap? Is it preventing you from taking risks, doing what you truly want, being vulnerable, engaging in intimate relationships, or going after your dreams?

3. Reason with yourself. Now it's time to get into Scientist mode and have a logical, practical conversation with yourself. Evaluate whether the payoff of avoidance (the benefit of avoiding the feeling or situation you identified in step 1) is greater than its cost (what it is preventing you from doing, as you identified in step 2). Is

avoiding disappointing someone else a better investment than speaking your truth? Is avoiding uncertainty worth not pursuing your greatest dreams? The answer should be a crystal-clear *no*. Realize the absurdity of your avoidance trap so you are inspired to get out of it.

4. Take a baby step. Once you realize what your avoidance trap is and what it is costing you, take action. Don't just think of what you want; take an action step toward it. Write down what you are committing to and when you will start moving toward it. Choose something you would not have done in the past because you were too busy trying to avoid something. For example, apply for a job you want. Ask your crush out on a date. And remember, this does not have to be a big, dramatic step — just one baby step at a time will eventually lead to larger leaps of faith.

· · · ·

YOUR CORE VALUES

"If you don't stick to your values when they're being tested,
they're not values: they're hobbies."
— Jon Stewart

Now that you have identified what has been keeping you trapped in your Expectation Hangovers, the next step is to redirect your attention to what you want to move toward so you can get unstuck. Our values are different from our superpowers: our values are things we want to develop and cultivate more of; our superpowers are intrinsic qualities that are already there and simply must be expressed. If you are not clear about your core values, you are more likely to be driven by expectations. When we replace expectations with values, we discover tremendous inspiration and enthusiasm to behave in accordance with them. When you know unequivocally what you value most, it gets easier to know what choices to make and actions to take so that your life becomes a reflection of the things that are most important to you.

COURTNEY'S STORY

I always knew I was going to grad school to get a master's in marketing research. I did everything possible to make that happen because it was critical to the life I "knew" I wanted. Financial security was important to me, and I wanted to avoid ever having to feel out of control. A plan was comforting. Then it all came crashing down. I was miserable in my program. I decided to quit. It was the scariest and most liberating time of my life. I was in such shock at the "destruction" of my life. I began to reevaluate my life plans, and piece by piece, it eventually clicked. I began to see the discrepancies between who I am and what I value, on the one hand, and what I had planned and pinned myself to achieving, on the other. I began to realize how the work I thought I wanted to do may have saved me from ever having to worry about money but wouldn't have ever matched up with my core values. So I started to focus solely on my number one value of making a difference and moved toward that. Today I love my job in human resources and do feel that I'm making a difference, which I learned is more valuable to me than a huge paycheck. The biggest takeaway that I had from my Expectation Hangover is that it's better to be guided by my values than by fear.

※ **EXERCISE**
Clarifying Your Core Values

With this exercise, you will create a specific and carefully thought-out list of the core values that govern your goals, and the choices and behaviors that support attaining them.

1. In your journal make a list of all the values you want to move toward. Write down everything that comes to mind — don't worry about. narrowing it down immediately. When creating your list, remember it is for *you*. Trust your gut and pick words, phrases, or concepts that feel enlivening, comprehensive, and meaningful to you rather than things you think should be on the list. Think of a person you admire and ponder what their values may be. If a value evokes specific pictures, feelings, and visions that truly resonate with what is most

important to you, then you are spot on! To get you started, here is a list of common core values: accountability, adventure, beauty, community, compassion, connection, contribution, creativity, discipline, empathy, excellence, faith, freedom, friendship, fun, independence, integrity, kindness, learning, love, loyalty, meaning, personal growth, respect, self-expression, service, tolerance, trust, truth, wisdom.

2. Once you've completed your list, you'll start to notice that certain values fit into a larger "big picture" value. For example, some of the items on my value list were family, friends, conversation, and love. I realized that all of these things were components of my number one core value: *connection*. Values like self-expression, joy, inspiration, and authenticity are part of *creativity*, and contribution and personal growth are part of *service*. Narrow your list down to five core values.

"My Expectation Hangovers have come not from disappointment with a difficult life event, but from a sense of failing myself and others because I'm not paying attention to where I'm headed, what I'm being drawn to, the choices I'm making. Empowering myself to make healthy choices that support my values and not settle for anything less than totally acceptable (in any relationship or situation) will go a long way toward helping me avoid this same pain in the future."

— Harrison

3. After you have identified your core values, display them where you can see them every day. The most successful companies display their core values and create teams, visions, and goals around them. Why don't we as individuals do the same so we can fully flourish in our own lives?

Anytime you observe yourself moving *away from* action because of your avoidance trap, shift your focus to what you want to move *toward*. I got out of my avoidance trap, which was based on fear of rejection, by focusing on connection, creativity, service, courage, and faith. What do you really want to experience in life? What can you spend *more* of your time and energy focusing on that will help you create what you want?

· · · ·

On an energetic level, *away from* motivation is like being physically pushed and comes with "shoulds" and "have tos." The energy of *toward* motivation is like something pulling us closer to what we want and comes with more "choose tos" and "want tos." Would you rather be pushed by pain or pulled by vision? Which feels better?

TRANSFORMATIONAL TRUTH
We Get Do-Overs

Sometimes we get to the other side of an Expectation Hangover with complete confidence that we've learned what we needed to learn to prevent the same kind of hangover, and then we face an almost identical one. What happened?

You did not fail at your treatment plan. The Universe often delivers a do-over to give us a chance to practice and fully embody healthier responses to Expectation Hangovers.

When Audrey's adult daughter Julie got into a relationship with her current boyfriend, Audrey felt she was losing her — physically and emotionally. Julie moved to a different state and dropped out of grad school to be with this man, much to her mother's disappointment. Audrey worked through her treatment plan and learned that her identity was intertwined with being a mom so much that when she felt left out of her children's lives, she felt lost and worthless. The blessing that came from her Expectation Hangover was finding her own sense of identity again. But when her other daughter surprised Audrey with the news that she would not be coming home for Christmas, Audrey felt an old, familiar hangover coming on about the expectations she had of her daughters. Thanks to the healthy way Audrey had learned to overcome similar disappointment, she only suffered the symptoms of an Expectation Hangover briefly; she was able to shift her thoughts easily; taking self-nurturing action was virtually effortless; and she was able to discover the lessons in this new hangover. Most important, she was able to accept her daughter's choice from a loving place rather than hanging on to wishing, hoping, and expecting it to be different.

Do-overs give us the opportunity to say no to something we may have said yes to in the past. Perhaps you tended to attract romantically unavailable people, only to be left with a huge Expectation Hangover when they did not commit. But then you did the work to move through your Expectation Hangover and are now crystal clear that you are no longer interested in dating unavailable people. All of a sudden, an attractive yet unavailable somebody comes into your life again. This is a chance for you to say no to that person so you can truly experience the lesson and integrate it into your life. Often the only way we can shift an old pattern is to be in a situation where we are experiencing it again but consciously and lovingly choose to respond differently. Welcome and embrace the do-overs!

Value-Inspired Action

"The journey of a thousand miles begins with one step."
— Lao-tzu

Now it is time to put all your theories together by committing to at least three value-aligned action steps to treat your Expectation Hangover. A value-aligned action step is one in which you are expressing your superpowers and cultivating your core values. It is imperative you do at least three things. Why three? Three is a powerful number because it is the first number that can form a plane (think of the three points of a triangle) and help a concept materialize. It signifies conception and manifestation; three has been called the most royal number, as it is solid, real, substantial, complete, and entire. Using the number three as symbolic of bringing your thoughts into form, synthesize everything you have learned so far by committing to three action steps.

Our superpowers give us momentum and allow us to fuel ourselves from a place of abundance; our core values give us the direction to move toward and help us get unstuck on the behavioral level. For instance, if one of your superpowers is creativity and a core value that you would like to cultivate is self-expression, possible action steps could be to paint for at least thirty minutes a day, sing every morning, or submit your manuscript to an agent. If your superpower is love and a value you'd like to move toward is connection, possible action steps could be calling a loved one each day, writing letters of gratitude to friends, or committing to going to at least one networking event per month with like-minded people. If your superpower is compassion and a value you want to move toward is empowerment, possible action steps could include setting boundaries with others as an act of self-care, treating yourself to a massage, or saying at least one kind thing to yourself out loud every day. Or if your superpower is intelligence and a value you'd like to move toward is success, possible action steps may be updating your résumé, requesting informational interviews with individuals who are successful in a way you admire, or setting a time to have a conversation with a mentor or supervisor.

✳ **EXERCISE**
Commitment Contract and Accountability Partner

A clear, specific commitment to your action steps is much more powerful than an expectation to achieve them. It's important that your focus be on making choices, based on your superpowers, that move you toward the values you want to cultivate. Your focus needs to be on taking the action, not an expectation of a particular outcome. Create a commitment contract with yourself right now that lists at least three action steps you will take that come from a place of inspiration. Make it official by printing the contract on a thick embossed-style paper (the kind diplomas are printed on) and design some kind of personal seal or graphic. Type out each commitment and begin each one with "I, [your name], commit to [your action step]." Sign and date your contract. Display it where you can see it. Be proud of your commitments!

You will be even more successful in honoring your commitments if you have an accountability partner. That person could be a coach, friend, or colleague. Choose someone you feel comfortable confiding in and who would not tolerate any excuses about why you did not keep your word to yourself. Share with them what your commitments are and when you plan to take an action step. Ask them to follow up with you on that date. Invite your partner to play along by offering to be an accountability partner back to him or her. Friends who play together in accountability stay together in integrity! If you do end up not following through on a commitment, do not go into resignation or self-criticism. Simply renegotiate your agreement with yourself by recommitting to a step. For instance, if you did not submit the five résumés you committed to submit by Friday, renegotiate with yourself and recommit to submitting them by the following Wednesday.

• • • •

Feeling Overwhelmed and Procrastinating

"You are your own worst enemy. If you can learn to stop expecting impossible perfection, in yourself and others, you may find the happiness that has always eluded you."
— Lisa Kleypas

You are probably going to feel a lot of inspiration and momentum regarding your action steps. But just in case you come up against the common road-blocks of feeling overwhelmed and procrastinating, I want to offer you ways to get through them.

We feel overwhelmed when we have a big or distant vision of something without knowing the steps to take to get there. Instead of moving into our proactive Scientist mode, we become paralyzed by having too much to do, and we feel incompetent or incapable of doing it. It's great to have a long-term vision, but if you are looking too far ahead, it is natural to feel over-whelmed because your brain is trying to process all the steps you have to take to get there. Imagine standing at the bottom of the staircase, staring up at the second floor and contemplating how you are going to get there. Rather than taking a running leap to see how many steps you can skip, and possibly twisting your ankle, you need to go step-by-step. The second you shift your focus from the destination (the second floor) to the first step in front of you, the feeling of being overwhelmed will disappear. Ask yourself, "What is one step I can take that is aligned with my long-term vision?"

You may be thinking, "But I don't know what my long-term vision is!" That's okay because all you need to know are the core values you want to experience. For instance, you may not know what career you want but know the type of things you'd like to be experiencing in your job. So if creativity

"I released the need to control every little detail of my life. It's much easier this way — having vision and taking one step toward it each day. I know where I want to end up, even though I do not know exactly how I will get there. I'm trusting the process."

— Paul

and collaborating with others are values, take an action step today that puts you in the energetic experience of being creative and collaborative, such as enrolling in improv classes or joining a volunteer committee. You do not have to figure everything out all at once — just take the first step.

When you find yourself up against the roadblock of procrastination, it is because your focus is too short term. By only looking at the steps that are necessary to take, you have lost touch with your *why*. Most of our heart-felt desires require some degree of effort that is not particularity fun, so we procrastinate. Not all value-aligned action steps are necessarily enjoyable; however, the underlying reason for taking them is what makes them aligned with our values. Shift your vision beyond the task at hand to why you are ultimately doing the task. Use Horseback Rider Rx to redirect your thoughts toward a positive future fantasy that inspires you. Instead of telling yourself you have to do something, tell yourself you choose to, get to, or want to do it because it is a step toward your core values and dreams.

For instance, if a core value is abundance and a dream is to travel, a value-aligned action step may be to create a budget. You may be putting off sitting in front of a computer and getting a reality check on your finances, but if you see that choosing to create a budget is ultimately moving you a step closer to something you really want, you will be more motivated to do it. Attuning to your *why* moves you from the seemingly mundane to the ulti-mately rewarding. Every big idea began with one small step, and every big shot started out as a little shot.

> "Vision is a destination — a fixed point to which we focus all effort.
> Strategy is a route — an adaptable path to get us where we want to go."
> — Simon Sinek

CONCLUSION

Epiphanies are priceless, yet wasted if not supported by action. Awareness plus action equals change. You are a cocreator with the Universe. In order to create the experiences you desire, you have to take a step in the direction you want to go. Ascension requires momentum. So unless you are going to be a monk and meditate on a mountaintop all day long, becoming passive and allowing all things to happen organically is not an option.

Stepping out of our comfort zone by taking new actions becomes more natural when we modify what is driving our behavior. Action that is inspired by a clear sense of who we are and by intentions that are in alignment with what we truly want may feel scary, but in an exciting rather than a paralyzing way. Remember: inspiration is the key to changing on the behavioral level. Without it, disappointment remains challenging and cumbersome to navigate.

Please don't lie to yourself and say, "But I don't know what to do." That's just not true. You are creative, wise, and completely capable of knowing something you can do right now to move yourself in the direction of your dreams. It may feel uncomfortable or scary at first, but that's great news because it means you are moving out of your comfort zone. Trust me, going for what you want and not getting it is wiser than never going for it at all. If you never go for it, you'll never know if you could have gotten it. If the result is another Expectation Hangover, so what? Now you are far more able to treat it. Chase your pleasure.

> "Inaction breeds doubt and fear.
> Action breeds confidence and courage. If you want to conquer fear,
> do not sit home and think about it. Go out and get busy."
> — Dale Carnegie

Chapter Nine

THE SPIRITUAL LEVEL

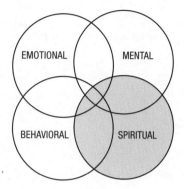

"Know that everything is in perfect order whether you understand it or not."
— Valery Satterwhite

From a spiritual perspective there is no such thing as disappointment. What we call disappointment, Spirit sees as opportunities for learning. While I would have loved to simply skip to this chapter and tell you there is really no such thing as disappointment, that would be a spiritual bypass. I'd be doing you a huge disservice because we are spiritual beings having a human experience, and disappointment feels unequivocally real. There is tremendous value in first working through our emotions, thoughts, and actions as they relate to Expectation Hangovers because then we are more open to moving into the profound shifts that occur on a spiritual level.

When I say "spiritual," I am not referring to any specific religion or doctrine, and I do not expect you to *take on* everything in this chapter. Your spirituality is sacred to you, and I respect that. At the very least, I invite you to *try on* the belief that there is an infinite loving force you are connected to, which you may call God, Lord, Spirit, Divine, Oneness, or even Nature, and that this Higher Power loves you very much. If you are like me, your

Expectation Hangover may have been the very thing that has opened or is opening your heart to developing a deeper spiritual life.

Let's begin with a brief review of what is at the basis of most spiritual teachings, which is this: we are all born aware that the very essence of our being is love. And then things happen that make us forget. We often disconnect from a Higher Power and feel separate. Spirituality is about returning to the place of original innocence and connection. Simply put, it is moving out of the energy of fear and back to love.

Returning to love is a *removing* and *remembering* process — it is not something you need to *learn* how to do. Expectation Hangovers become a spiritual tool because the more we allow ourselves to be who we truly are rather than holding rigidly to who we have been expected to be, the less we have the kind of strong reactions that create disappointment. The more connected we feel to a Higher Power, the easier it becomes to release expectations and hold on to faith.

> "Love is the essential reality and our purpose on earth. To be consciously aware of it, to experience love in ourselves and others, is the meaning of life. Meaning does not lie in things. Meaning lies in us."
> — Marianne Williamson

THE GOAL LINE VERSUS THE SOUL LINE

At the University of Santa Monica (where I earned my master's degree in spiritual psychology and currently serve on the faculty), we learn and teach that there are two lines of life: the goal line and the soul line. The goal line is everything that happens in our life that takes place in the external physical reality. It includes our money, jobs, actions, body, relationships, possessions, and so on. The soul line corresponds to our "spiritual curriculum," composed of life lessons we are here to learn and the evolution of our internal awareness.

The goal line is like a horizontal line: there is not a clear final destination. We simply move forward on the goal line in a constant pursuit of more, better, or different, attempting to fulfill ourselves through external things. When things go awry on the goal line, we find ourselves with — you guessed it — an Expectation Hangover.

There is no final destination or end game on the soul line because we are never really "there." But there is a distinct direction we are headed on the soul line: toward Love. And not the love for or from someone or something, but the big love that is the essence of each one of us, Agape Love. Allow me to clarify that we absolutely feel love for people and things on the goal line. Yet there is a place inside each one of us that can only be touched from within.

The soul line is where we evolve in our consciousness and embark on a journey of returning to love. What do I mean by "evolving in conscious-ness"? This is not just some woo-woo jargon; it is actually physics. When you release experiences, emotions, judgments, thoughts, behaviors, and old patterns that have been based in fear, you literally change the electromagnetic vibration of your body. As you let go of expectations and your attachments to them, you literally become lighter. Be-cause our Expectation Hangovers hit us hardest on the goal line, we find our way to the soul line almost by default. Nothing has catapulted my spiritual evolution more than disappointment because it has shown me where I have been most invested on the goal line. Through the painful experience of feel-ing lost, I found my way to the soul line.

"I have a newfound source of compassion and love for others because of my own painful struggles and experiences. I am a living example that you can get out, move forward, and things will be okay."

— Greg

Now here is the part to get really excited about: as we resolve issues on the soul line that have triggered or reinforced Expectation Hangovers, life on the goal line becomes a lot more graceful and synchronistic. Soon you will marvel at how many opportunities flow into your life that are more in alignment with your most heartfelt dreams and desires.

"The most beautiful people we have known are those who have known defeat, known suffering, known struggle, known loss, and have found their way out of the depths. These persons have an appreciation, a sensitivity, and an understanding of life that fills them with compassion, gentleness, and a deep loving concern. Beautiful people do not just happen."
— Elisabeth Kübler-Ross

Since we are spiritual beings having a human experience, we cannot live entirely on the soul line because it would be impossible to pay our bills and feed ourselves. Not to mention all the fun human things we are blessed to be able to do, like creating art, connecting with loved ones, and traveling to beautiful places. The goal line is not negative, for it is where we get to celebrate our gifts and share our love with others. The happiest and most content people I have come across are those who, although aware the goal line is a wonderful part of the human experience, are dedicated to their journey on the soul line. In our modern world the path of the mind is separating more and more from the path of the heart. Moving our awareness to the soul line helps bring them together again. Treating Expectation Hangovers on the spiritual level is a disintegration process that moves you from separation of the goal line and soul line into a process of integrating them, which allows you to experience yourself as a spiritual being.

YOUR SPIRITUAL CURRICULUM

"I am learning that everything is for me and that Spirit knows better than I do what is best for me. Now to get my ego to move into acceptance and cooperation with that. I am aware today that this is the shortest path to freedom and really the only way of opening to and expanding into what is next for me."
— Paula Majeski

What if life really were one big classroom where all the lessons you learned were specifically designed to help you grow on the soul line? A classroom where you were never good or bad and there was no concept of right or wrong. And where you felt loved and never alone. Wouldn't that be a pretty cool classroom? I'd like to go to school there, wouldn't you? Well guess what — we are all students at this school!

Although there are some common lessons, we all have our own unique curriculum that consists of the events, people, and Expectation Hangovers that teach us what our soul is seeking to learn. All our life lessons come bearing the gift of wisdom. We miss this gift when we begin to identify with the challenge or setback as who we are. We are far greater than we can imagine; but we doubt, and we allow the current circumstances of our Expectation Hangover to dictate our possibilities. Knowing that life is indeed like one big classroom and we are all here to learn can transform you. This is much different than the American Dream of status, power, and money. By seeing our lives this way, there are no mistakes, no failures, no victims — just gifts and opportunities for spiritual growth and connection.

> "What's happening is merely what's happening.
> How you feel about it is another matter."
> — Neale Donald Walsch

I understand that these concepts may be hard to swallow because your mind could make a great argument that there have been some pretty brutal things that have happened to you that felt more like punishment than a lesson. You may also object by saying there are definitely things in the world that are bad or wrong: war, disease, poverty, crime, cruelty, and injustice, to name just a few. And you are absolutely correct that there are things in this world that feel tragic, unfair, and even unbearable. You may even have had an Expectation Hangover that has felt that way. The truth I am inviting you to consider is that from a spiritual perspective, there is no evaluation of or opinion about what happens.

At forty Edie lost her husband and found herself a single mother to her eleven-year-old son. For quite a while she walked around in a numbing fog. The adjustment to being widowed after being part of a team was intense. Then she heard "the voice of God" tell her to finish the work that her husband hadn't been able to finish, and she became a motivational teacher and Reiki master. Here's how Edie describes her transformation:

> I would go through rounds of anger, but I knew I needed to move forward in my life and turn it into something healing for myself and others. As a result, I also became an organ-donor educator. Much of what I teach and write about is resilience and thriving in the face of major life change. I learned that love is never wasted; that everyone is on loan to us; that everyone we know and love will one day die or leave us, or we will die or leave them. All of those things are cause for celebration rather than despair, and this helps me appreciate the people in my life.

Most of us judge far more often than we accept. But acceptance is the first law of spirit, so if we desire to live a life based on love rather than fear, we must stop judging as much as possible. Now, does that mean we have to like everyone and agree with everything? Does it mean we just take everything that comes our way even if we do not like it? No, no, no. We still have discernment, which is about preferences. When we discern, we are simply saying yes or no, without all the internal commentary. Judgment is charged because it entails a feeling of "against" or "for." To explain discernment, I like to use the analogy of going to a buffet. When you go to a buffet, you look around, put some things you want to eat on your plate, and leave the rest behind. You do not react with disgust to the things you choose not to put on your plate. You don't think, "Look at that awful potato salad! Get that off the buffet — it shouldn't be here!" Instead, you just pass on it. And that's true discernment. We all have our own little judgers in our head who believe they are protecting and assisting us with all their opinions. But they're not.

When you free yourself from right/wrong thinking regarding your Expectation Hangover, you move through your life lessons more quickly. If you don't pick up the meaning of a particular lesson, you may feel stuck with it until you discover the gift or teaching it holds. Judgment keeps us in either a controlling or a victim consciousness because we see the world as happening either *by* us or *to* us rather than *for* us. When we approach our Expectation Hangovers from the elevated perspective that everything is really happening for us as part of our spiritual curriculum, we no longer see our disappointment as a form of punishment, misfortune, or failure.

LYDIA'S STORY

I contracted a virus while teaching fourth grade, and my body essentially fell apart. I was diagnosed with countless diseases and eventually had to face the fact that I would have to give up my teaching career. Although it hasn't been easy, I have learned to look at every disappointment and heartbreak as a chance to grow and become a stronger person. When your life is turned upside down, it can be a very dark place. I could have chosen to brace myself for the terrifying roller coaster of a chronic health battle. I could have focused on the lonely hospital nights or the map of scars covering my body. Instead, I realized that with every obstacle in life, I have a choice. I made the choice to embrace my life. I chose gratitude over devastation, and I make that choice every single day. I returned to school to become a certified health coach. I help my clients learn to blossom from within and make lifestyle and dietary changes to reclaim their health and happiness.

Turns out I did regain my life, but not exactly as I had planned. I learned that regaining your health and happiness has little to do with receiving a diagnosis and taking a pill. Instead, it comes from a place of laughing at life's many quirks, indulging in nature's pharmacy, accepting and loving your innermost thoughts, and approaching each day with an abundance of gratitude. My Expectation Hangover reshaped my future and forced me to dive deep and learn what I am really made of.

ROLE-PLAYING Rx: THE SEEKER

To treat your Expectation Hangover on the spiritual level, take on the role of the Seeker and explore the classroom of your life. Now, you may be wondering why the role-playing Rx here is not that of a student, given that life is a series of lessons. Yes, a student studies and learns, but a seeker wants even more. By stepping into the role of the Seeker, you discover the lessons of your Expectation Hangover, go toward love rather than goal-line results, and ask for the assistance of your Higher Self and Spirit rather than thinking you need to figure things out with your mind and do it all on your own. As a Seeker, call upon the spirit of adventure and be willing to be shown a new direction. Prepare to traverse the terrain of the soul line. It is the territory of the unknown, the mystical, and the magical. It is the road less traveled because it takes great courage to identify less with the goal line.

We immediately become the Seeker when we ask, "Why is this happening *for* me, and what am I learning?" rather than "Why is this happening *to* me?" We then move into the energy of curiosity, avoid falling into patterns of hopelessness and helplessness, and discover the miracles in our life. Consider that a miracle is a change in perception, which makes creating miracles easy for all of us. Change your perception and be willing to see that the Universe is *for* you, not *against* you.

An overachiever, Kyle was successful in various areas of his life; this included being a finalist on a reality-TV competition and securing a high-profile job in a corporation. One day all the doing caught up with him, and he quit pursuing both paths. Once the relief wore off, panic set it. His compensatory strategy kicked into high gear as he felt the need to go out and do more. He sought help to figure out the direction for the next chapter of his life on the goal line, but our work together was really about the soul line. Each time we talked, Kyle would tell me about how he felt fear when he thought of pursuing a path and when he thought of not pursuing anything. He was both afraid of making the "wrong" choice and afraid not to choose at all.

Kyle explored the fear and discovered that a longing for some kind of spiritual connection was beneath it. His entire life had been about *doing* so he could feel he was in control of something and distract himself from the panic he experienced whenever he felt he didn't know something. He lived on fear, not faith. As Kyle courageously explored his fears and the issues in his life that made him feel he needed to be in control, he discovered a deeper, wiser part of himself. He came to know himself as a human *being* rather than just a human *doing*. Through a consistent practice of meditation, Kyle also began to experience more peace, connectedness, and intuition. His Expectation Hangover was the doorway to a completely different relationship with himself and Spirit.

By taking on the role of the Seeker, Kyle was able to communicate with his own intuition. Our intuition is full of infinite wisdom and possesses a consciousness beyond the ego, which is primarily invested in instant gratification. Our ego will try to problem-solve so we can fix whatever is wrong and stop any feelings of discomfort. A Seeker has patience and will take time to discover the lessons.

"Meditation is listening to the Divine within."
— Edgar Cayce

✤ **GUIDED VISUALIZATION**
Connecting to Yourself as a Spiritual Being

You can download the audio version of this exercise at
www.expectationhangover.com/bonus

When we're immersed in the noise of an Expectation Hangover, it can be difficult to hear the voice of our intuition and Spirit. So the Seeker supports us in quieting the mind enough to listen. Through practices like this visualization exercise, we can experience greater peace and clarity internally, even when our external world feels like it is in chaos. Read all the directions so you understand them, then take yourself through the exercise.

1. Find a quiet, comfortable place to sit where you won't be interrupted. Sit with your feet on the floor.

2. Close your eyes and take three very, very deep breaths. Slowly inhale and exhale. Focus on your breath, and notice where it is stopping. Are you breathing deeply, or is your breath stopping at your throat or your chest?

3. Elongate your breath so you are breathing all the way down to your toes. Feel your feet on the floor; focus on the sound of your breath. Put your shoulders back and down. Relax. Notice the position of your head. If your chin is down, move it a little so it's lifted and in a neutral position. Soften your jaw; relax your eyelids and eyebrows; and just listen to and feel your breath. Become totally present.

4. Shift your awareness to your feet; feel your connection to the earth and your physical body. Scan your physical body and notice where there may be any tension or a sensation of heaviness. Imagine that everything that no longer serves you — any cares, concerns, judgments, beliefs, or burdens you are carrying — is emptying out through the bottoms of your feet. See Mother Earth taking everything you no longer need. You do not have to know what you are releasing; visualize letting it go through the bottoms of your feet.

"My Expectation Hangover taught me that I am worthy. It's been a long time since I thought that, and for a while I thought I would never feel worthy of anything again. The biggest blessing has been the wake-up call of 'Hey you! You are someone! You are great! Now go share it with the world!' Without this experience I probably would have continued walking through life with my fear-based beliefs and closed mind."

— Jamie

5. Stay present and begin shifting your focus up through your physical body. Begin at your feet, then move up through your legs, your hips, your abdomen, your chest, your shoulders, your neck, your head, and the top of your head.

6. Expand that awareness out three feet around you, then another three feet, and another three feet, expanding, expanding, expanding. Feel yourself opening outward and connecting; feel that lightness, that expansiveness, that oneness. Begin experiencing yourself as a spiritual being. Feel the connection to a Higher Power that you always have access to.

7. Keeping that expansiveness, begin to bring your awareness to your heart, which is the intersection of your physical reality, or goal line, and your inner spiritual world, or soul line. See these two worlds integrating. Experience yourself as a spiritual being having a human experience.

8. Move one hand to your heart, breathe in, and say several things to yourself that are deeply loving, such as "I love you," "You are not alone," "I am here," "You are connecting," "All is well," "There is only Love." Just feel into Agape Love; this is who you truly are. Right here, in this right place, in this moment, there is no Expectation Hangover. Take another nice, deep breath.

9. When you are ready, slowly open your eyes and bring your awareness back into the room.

. . . .

LIVING INSIDE OUT

"As long as anyone believes that his ideal and purpose is outside him,
that it is above the clouds, in the past or in the future,
he will go outside himself and seek fulfillment where it cannot be found.
He will look for solutions and answers at every point
except where they can be found — in himself."
— Erich Fromm

During the height of my many Expectation Hangovers, I would begin sessions with my coach feeling depressed, anxious, or an uncomfortable combination of both. I blamed my state of discontent on the fact that things in my life just were not going the way I wanted. If only I could find my soul mate or a career I could be passionate about, then I would feel confident, happy, and fulfilled. My coach would say, "None of that matters or will make any difference if you get it. You gotta live in-out and not out-in!" At the time, it was so frustrating to hear because I just wanted her to tell me the answer that would make me feel better. You see, at that time I did not have the patience of a Seeker.

Most of us live a bit backward. The outer circumstances of life become the conductor of our thoughts, feelings, and behaviors. And once we've boarded this out-in train, we enter a cycle of looking for something on the outside to ease the uneasiness inside. What we are truly searching for is a sense of inner contentment, no matter what is or isn't happening in our outside world. Contentment is actually our natural state because from a soul-line perspective, nothing is missing.

> "Losing what I thought was 'everything' taught me that the real 'everything' I ever wanted is already inside me. All the information, the love, the acceptance, the motivation, the passion is there, waiting to be ignited."
> — Gloria

We just forget this because we get so fixated on the goal line, where there is an infinite supply of distractions that we *think* will lead to fulfillment.

This does not mean that we should minimize or not enjoy the things in our external world. I experience a deep sense of personal fulfillment after facilitating a workshop and witnessing people's transformation. I am filled with joy when I call my young nephew and hear him say, "I love you, Auntie" in his cute little voice. I am uplifted by time with my friends when we are laughing. And I feel a great sense of satisfaction when I accomplish something like finishing a book or completing a challenging workout. However, I do not rely on those external things to be the source of my internal state.

Everything you desire is within you. It's actually rather ironic: Spirit places the things we most desire closest to us so they are easy to find, but it's the last place we look! You will not only understand, but *embody*, this if you reorient yourself from out-in to in-out. I want you to think of a time in your life when you felt total elation, a time you felt really joyful. As you recall the memory, feel the joy, the love, the smile on your face, the connection you experienced. Bring all the qualities you were feeling at that time fully into your awareness. Are you feeling it? Please do not continue reading until you bring forward those amazing feelings you felt. I want you to be aware of your ability to bring all those feelings forward simply with a memory. The truth is you were not having the experience, but you were able to generate joy. That is because the joy lives in you. The memory merely elicited the joy that lives inside you.

KATIE'S STORY

I always wanted to escape the small town in Oklahoma where I grew up and move to New York City. I knew if I could just get to a more inspired city, then everything I ever wanted would be available to me. So I left everything I knew, with two suitcases and a few hundred dollars. Although I am happy to say my time in New York City consisted of many good memories and life-changing experiences, it wasn't exactly the Sex and the City *solution I expected.*

It took me a while to realize this because, on the outside, everything looked pretty good — I had a cute apartment, a good job, and many opportunities. My ego soared as I moved up in the world and lived the "glamorous" lifestyle I had dreamed of. However, none of this ultimately mattered because underneath the sparkly exterior was a girl with an intense Expectation Hangover. Despite the impression I gave the world, I felt the same way I did back home — lost, insecure, and not good enough. Slowly but surely, my sparkly exterior began to crack. I was going into debt, making bad choices, and becoming more and more depressed. I was in the "greatest city in the world," and all I did was sit in my apartment watching TV. The best way to sum up what my Expectation Hangover taught me is the saying "Wherever you go, there you are." I thought that I could outrun my insecurities and weaknesses, but I actually needed to look at them with compassion and allow them to heal.

I put my ego aside and asked what my soul really needed, and it was clear that it was time to move back to Oklahoma and build a more solid foundation. I have gotten so much more clarity about what I want and who I want to be. I still don't know exactly what and how it will all work out, but I know that I never want to look outside myself for the answers. A question that really helps me remember what is important is, "If I removed all the expectations and comparisons, what would really matter to me?"

⬥ **TOOL**
Forgiveness

"Forgiveness is the fragrance a violet sheds on the heel that has crushed it."
— Mark Twain

I consider forgiveness a tool to use on the spiritual level because I have found that it is the most spiritual thing we do as humans. Yet it is often underused because it is misunderstood. Since we have been conditioned to be externally focused, we have gotten into the bad habit of blaming someone else, ourselves, or a combination of both for our Expectation Hangovers.

Most Expectation Hangovers tend to come with a cast of characters that, from our perspective, played a role in delivering disappointment. Our egos get really attached to being right, which often perpetuates blame, resentment, and holding on to grudges. We resist forgiving because we believe we were wronged and think we need to hold on to our judgments of a person or situation to feel justified. What is key to understand about forgiveness is that it is not about letting someone else off the hook — it is about setting *you* free. Forgiveness does not mean we are agreeing with or condoning what happened. Forgiveness does mean we are letting go of the judgments we've been harboring inside. Also, when it comes to forgiving someone else, it is not something that has to be done face-to-face with anyone, nor does the other person have to forgive us to be forgiven. Forgiveness is something we do inside ourselves.

"Forgiveness helped me to believe in myself; to awaken in consciousness; to take care of myself on all levels; to recognize that I could not and would not ever 'fix' anyone other than myself; to let go of judgments that I failed; to let go of resentment and judgment held against others; to know my truth; and to believe in love again, starting with myself, in a whole new way."
— Joanne

I invite you to set yourself free by seeing the people in your life, including those you judged as harming you, from the perspective of a Seeker. Be willing to see their life curriculum and know that they have experienced things that have been painful. Their Expectation Hangovers have triggered behavior that may have been the source of yours. People who seemingly harm others are coming from a place of profound disconnection. Everyone is truly doing the best they can. Even if you feel passionately that they knew better or could do better, it is unreasonable to expect people to act the way we would have acted in a similar situation. To ascend on the soul line, we must be willing to drop our expectations of others and forgive them for any suffering we have accused them of causing. Be a Seeker rather than a victim by seeing their pain and having compassion for their human experience rather than holding on to pain and blame.

June's mother was an alcoholic, and all her life June tried to find ways to get her sober. Each day, June awoke hoping that it would be the day her mom stopped drinking. And each day, she was disappointed because her mother didn't stop. June never stood up for herself when her mother insulted her or criticized her life because she thought that if she hurt her mother's feelings, she would just drink more. If June sought out help, her mother would not talk to her for months. Over the years, June had a chronic Expectation Hangover because her mother was not the mother she wished for. June struggled with depression, built up resentment, and spent a lot of time alone because it was challenging for her to trust anyone.

Recently, through another family member, June learned that her mother had a terrible childhood full of abuse and that her own mother drank to excess when she was pregnant. As she got the full picture of her mother's life curriculum, June was able to see that her alcoholism was a result of her childhood. The grand lesson June learned when she shifted to the perspective of a Seeker was that her mom was doing the best she could, given where she had come from. June was then able to forgive her mother and accept and love her for how and where she is on her life's journey. Forgiveness has been the key to recovering from a forty-year-old hangover. June says, "I learned to drop expectations and to just forgive. My Expectation Hangover taught me I can unconditionally love my mother for who she is. I can see the good in her. I feel free from negative thoughts and self-sabotaging behavior. There will be no more harsh judgments or unrealistic expectations coming from me. The biggest blessing is that I feel peaceful and joyous."

Instead of holding on to blame or feelings of rejection, move into appreciation of the "soul mates" who have come into your life to teach you valuable lessons about love. That's right, a soul mate isn't some magical person who sweeps you off your feet and completes you (I guess I won't be hired to write any chick-flick movie scripts anytime soon). There is no "one" because everyone who comes in and out of our life is the perfect one for what we are supposed to learn. Forgiving all of our soul mates is an act of self-love. The ones you feel hurt you the most are most often the ones who give you the greatest gift of all: an opportunity to create a more loving relationship with yourself.

> "Love yourself first and everything else falls into line.
> You really have to love yourself to get anything done in this world."
> — Lucille Ball

. . . .

DANA'S STORY

He turned to me, held my hand, looked me in the eyes (his eyes filled with tears), and he said, "I don't love you, and I don't know if I ever will." With those few words my world came crashing down. This man was the first person I spoke to every day and the last person I spoke to when I put my head on my pillow at night. He has four wonderful daughters who made me smile every day. This relationship was my rock, and it was my light and the love that filled my heart. It had all gone dark and was shattered. I struggled with depression, suicidal thoughts, and anxiety. I cried and cried and cried. I went through each day completely numb. I focused on everything I thought I wasn't. Was I not pretty enough? Not skinny enough? Not kind enough? Not smart enough? Did I not love him enough? Love his kids enough? My head was a huge mess. I went back through every minute and every day of our relationship, trying to determine what I did wrong: What didn't I do? What didn't I say? What did I say? How could he not love me? How on earth did I mess up?

I had a wake-up call when a coworker said to me, "You really have not broken up, because you are still in a relationship with him in your mind by trying to figure out what you did wrong. Let him go by forgiving yourself— and him." She suggested writing a forgiveness letter (that I would never mail) as a way to release him and myself. At first, I resisted because I was still holding on to some small bit of hope. I put off writing the letter because it felt so terminal. Finally one day I did it. I sat down to write the letter with a clear intention to set us both free and forgive. I wrote about my anger and sadness and what I wished would have happened. Then all the lessons I learned and experiences we shared that I was grateful for got clearer. I wrote what I was forgiving him for and what I forgave myself for. And I finally let go — not just of the grief about it ending, but also of the fantasy about it ever coming back. All the space that was being taken up with hurt, judgment, and expectation was now filled with forgiveness. I was flooded with compassion for us both. For the first time in a long time, I felt free. This breakup taught me that I truly do have the capacity to love, I am love, and I am loved unconditionally! Today I treat myself with love and compassion. I am better prepared now to handle any hangover and forgive myself, learn from it, and move on.

"There was literally a point where I tried to think of one single thing I liked about myself and came up empty. Even though my friends and family were sympathetic and forgiving toward me, I was not yet able to give myself that same unconditional love. The biggest blessing from my Expectation Hangover is that I learned that mistakes are simply a part of life, yet it is how we deal with them that can really have an impact. At first, I dealt with my mistakes by being mean to myself and incredibly regretful. Once I learned to forgive myself and be unconditionally loving to myself, I was able to see my mistake as a great learning opportunity, and everything shifted for me."

— Angela

Often the person we have the hardest time forgiving is ourself. Plagued by regret, we buy into the misunderstanding that if we forgive ourselves, we may be letting ourselves off the hook. Or that we will not learn the lesson we need to learn. This could not be further from the truth. We all make so-called mistakes. The process of forgiveness recognizes that we are all humans doing the best we can at any moment in spite of the fact that our performance falls short of our expectations. Please release the expectation that you are supposed to get it "right" all the time. If you continue to beat yourself up, treating an Expectation Hangover is not possible because you cannot transform when you are still harboring judgments.

You are ready to forgive. You have called upon the Surfer, who has supported you in working through feelings such as anger, resentment, sadness, and shame. The Horseback Rider has reined in your thoughts so you do not get stuck in a cycle of blameful or guilt-ridden thoughts and has helped you reframe your beliefs in a way that keeps you out of victimville. The Scientist has assisted you in altering behaviors, setting boundaries, and taking value-inspired action. It is now time to call upon the Seeker to give you the spiritual altitude you need to set yourself free.

The Seeker is here to help you understand that no one can actually *make* us feel anything! We choose our inner response to everything in our life, and holding on to all that anger and harboring resentment against others offer no relief from our Expectation Hangovers. Remember, every person is a fellow student in the classroom of life, and we are all helping each other, sometimes in seemingly painful ways, with our spiritual curriculum.

To be effective at using this power tool of forgiveness, there are two key points to understand. First, what we are actually forgiving ourselves for is judgments we have made against ourselves. And we forgive others (including Spirit) for judgments we have made against them. We are also forgiving ourselves for misunderstandings we have formed or limiting beliefs we have bought into about ourselves, someone else, or life. We are not really forgiving the events. Remember, on the soul line, where the Seeker resides, there is no such thing as good or bad — there is only what happened. Second, just saying a bunch of words in our head about how we forgive something will not release judgments and the toxic emotions that go with them. The energy underneath our words when forgiving must be compassion. Compassion is unconditional love and acceptance. It's not feeling sorry for; it's not trying to fix or change; it's just being a loving presence.

> "Life is an adventure in forgiveness."
> — Norman Cousins

✳ EXERCISE
Compassionate Self-Forgiveness

You can download the audio version of this exercise at
www.expectationhangover.com/bonus

To truly experience inner freedom, we must not harbor ill will toward anyone, including ourselves. It is the Seeker within all of us who knows that

Love is our essence, and anything that blinds us to seeing this must be dissolved so we are free to be who we truly are. Forgiveness is the doorway to that freedom. This exercise is adapted from the soul-centered basic skill "Facilitating Compassionate Self-Forgiveness" from the University of Santa Monica.

1. Find a quiet, comfortable place to sit where you won't be interrupted. You will be saying things out loud, so it is important you have your privacy. It may be helpful to refer back to your Expectation Hangover Assessment Form (p. 28) and Your Storyboard (p. 72) to bring forward beliefs and experiences that would be liberating to forgive.

2. Refer back to the visualization exercise Connecting with Your Own Compassion (p. 52) to cultivate the feeling of compassion. Feel the compassion that you would direct toward someone you unconditionally love, and as you begin to experience it, turn it toward yourself. Anything we feel toward another, we can feel toward ourselves.

3. Once you are experiencing self-compassion, you are ready to move into forgiveness by forgiving yourself for judgments you have made against yourself and others, as well as forgiving yourself for misunderstandings and limiting beliefs you have bought into. Use the following sentence stems to form self-forgiveness statements that you will say one by one out loud (it is important to use the exact wording so you capture the essence of forgiving judgments):

    I forgive myself for judging myself as... (For example: I forgive myself for judging myself as undesirable and unsuccessful.)

    I forgive myself for judging...as...(For example: I forgive myself for judging my mother as critical.)

    I forgive myself for judging myself for... (For example: I forgive myself for judging myself for cheating.)

    I forgive myself for judging...for...(For example: I forgive myself for judging my father for never being there for me.)

    I forgive myself for buying into the misunderstanding that... (For example: I forgive myself for buying into the misunderstanding that I am a failure because I lost my job.)

I forgive myself for buying into the limiting belief that…(For example: I forgive myself for buying into the limiting belief that I did something wrong and I am being punished.)

4. Say all your self-forgiveness statements out loud, as that is powerful and this is your power tool. Don't just say the words; feel them. Use your intuition to guide you through this process. You may be learning this tool for the first time. Go slow. Relieve yourself of the expectation to forgive every judgment you've ever made. Know this power tool is always available in your life's tool kit. Feel the waves of compassion wash over you. Keep saying these self-forgiveness statements until you experience a positive shift in your energy.

• • • •

Letting go of judgment liberates us from pain and the illusion of separation. What feels as though it has been lost returns when you forgive yourself, accept your human process, and free the power that has been locked in your judgment-based emotions, thoughts, and actions.

SURRENDERING TO A HIGHER POWER

"Some people believe holding on and hanging in there are signs
of great strength. However, there are times when it takes
much more strength to know when to let go and then do it."
— Ann Landers

What I've learned by coaching people is that Expectation Hangovers hit us in our most tender areas (often repeatedly). For example, people who long to be in healthy romantic partnerships experience pain involving breakups, betrayals in relationships, and not finding love, whereas people who are content in their love lives are usually disappointed with something else, such as their career.

This isn't some cruel joke from the Universe — remember that Expectation Hangovers don't happen to punish us! They keep recurring because sometimes it takes getting hit where it hurts the most to wake us up. Most people don't come to me for help because everything in their life is going great. They come because their Expectation Hangover has brought them to their knees and they are seeking a different path.

Surrender is one of those sexy spiritual words that is a pain in the you-know-what to practice when we are not getting what we want. We don't like it when the Universe seems to miss the memo on how we think things should be — in fact, it's the very thing that challenges our faith the most. But the truth is, the Universe doesn't miss anything. Your Expectation Hangover has brought you to your own personal wall, the edge of what you knew yourself to be. Instead of focusing on how big the obstacle is, or how impossible something may seem, lay down your will and surrender to the will of something greater. That may be God, or the Divine, or the Source, or Spirit, or Allah — the name doesn't matter; all that matters is that you connect back with your Higher Power.

"I feel like the Universe stepped in and knew that I needed a little assistance. When everything essentially fell apart, I was opened up to a place where I didn't feel like I had a choice any longer — I had to let go of what I thought I wanted and move forward to find myself."
— Hannah

The Seeker recognizes the value of surrender, of letting Spirit lead and relying less on the mind and directives from our expectations. We don't have to navigate life all by ourselves. There is so much support and guidance available to us from Spirit, but without surrender, it is impossible to take full advantage of it. The loneliness of Expectation Hangovers can propel us into establishing or deepening a relationship with a Higher Power. Most human beings experience longing. We think it's a longing for a soul mate or a life purpose, but ultimately, we all long to feel the connection to Spirit that we were born with.

I am not saying you shouldn't long for love or a career that lights your fire. Those things are *wonderful*. What I am saying is that the Universe may be giving you an advanced course in surrender right now to deepen your connection to your Higher Power. Make this a time to find the truest source of Love, comfort, and meaning that there is. Don't neglect the opportunity to admit a Divine influence into your life.

MARY'S STORY

When I was thirty-one years old, I married the man of my dreams, and within our first year of marriage, I was diagnosed with cancer. The news of the cancer spun my life around and took me in a completely new direction. My sense of spirituality broadened; I became a spiritual seeker, and my life paradigm shifted. I was led away from a life of toxic habits to a life of holistic healing. I began to meditate. I chose to forgive people in my life. One avenue led to another, which led to another. While it was traumatic and scary, it taught me what is important. I learned that love is the most important thing; that I am worthy of all good things; that God fully supports me; and that life can be good no matter what — *we just have to choose the way we see a certain situation. I also learned I could let go and trust God. The spiritual maturity that I've developed has been the biggest blessing of my Expectation Hangover. I'm a completely different person; I see life differently and have a renewed perspective. I did a 180, from being a default pessimist to being an eternal optimist. Of course, I have bad days sometimes, but now I have the tools, like meditation and prayer, to turn it around. I trust that God has my back and that His plans are for my Highest Good. It's so incredibly liberating and brings me such a sense of peace!*

✤ GUIDED VISUALIZATION
Surrender as a Spiritual Practice

You can download the audio version of this exercise at *www.expectationhangover.com/bonus*

This is a sacred process of surrendering, so take the time to create the space to experience this exercise fully. During this visualization exercise you will be engaging in physical movement that will help you connect with a Higher Power. Make sure you are undisturbed and have a quiet place to go on this inward journey. You will also need a candle. Read all the directions so you understand them, then take yourself through the exercise.

1. Before you begin, light the candle and ask, "May only that which is for my Highest Good come forward."
2. Sit either on the floor or in a chair with your spine straight. Rest your hands on your lap with your palms facing up. Do not cross or touch your hands at all.

3. Close your eyes and take five to ten deep, slow breaths in this receptive position.

4. Bring your awareness to the very top of your head. As you do, you might feel a tingling sensation along your scalp. Start to expand your awareness up and up and up. Take it three feet above your head, then another three feet, and keep expanding and expanding. Feel into your invisible connection to a Higher Power. Keep breathing.

5. Now with this expanded awareness, begin to bring to mind your Expectation Hangover and all the disappointment, cares, and concerns that go along with it. Imagine you are holding your Expectation Hangover, and all the symptoms that go with it, in your hands. Really see it. What color is it? What shape does it have? Maybe it's gray and wiry, or maybe it's a bright red box. Whatever you see is fine; trust your intuition to guide you.

6. Now really feel the weight of this Expectation Hangover in your hands. Feel the heaviness of it. Keep seeing the image, the color and shape, and imagine it getting bigger and bigger, heavier and heavier. Allow yourself to fully experience the weight of the Expectation Hangover that is burdening you. Keep breathing.

7. Now you are going to move into a sacred process of surrendering your Expectation Hangover to Spirit. To do so, gently and very slowly begin to physically lift your hands, which have been holding on to all your disappointment, cares, and concerns. As your hands rise, continue to see the image and feel the heaviness of your Expectation Hangover. Keep lifting and lifting your hands and arms until they are extended above your head and hold them there. Feel the discomfort. Allow yourself to physically experience the pain of carrying your Expectation Hangover.

8. When you have had enough and are ready to let go, imagine that a column of white light is descending upon you and removing the burden of your Expectation Hangover from your hands like a spiritual vacuum cleaner. See the color and shape of your Expectation Hangover being lifted into the light and slowly taken out of your hands. Feel the new lightness in your hands. Gradually and naturally, allow your arms to descend back onto your lap. Feel the lightness that

surrender creates. You do not have to hold on to so much. You can let go. It is safe to surrender. This is the process of letting go and "letting God."

9. Feel yourself being taken care of by a Higher Power. Allow this process of handing over to be a way that you establish and nourish your personal connection to Spirit.

10. To complete this process say "Thank you" inwardly and take a deep breath into your heart area. Breathe in the light and love that are always available to you.

11. When you are ready, slowly open your eyes and bring your awareness back into the room.

Repeat this meditation whenever your Expectation Hangover feels like too much to bear.

• • • •

Kasey had freed herself from an Expectation Hangover regarding her career (she ended up resigning from a "dream job" because of a toxic work environment). Recently, Kasey felt torn between being extremely proactive to make things happen and allowing herself the space to let things come naturally. When she pushes herself to "figure things out," she feels overwhelmed and anxious, and then shuts down; but when she errs on the passive side, she feels she isn't doing enough and fears missing out on opportunities because she's not taking action.

This is very common. We work hard to make things happen until we are so exhausted that we give ourselves a break. And then, once we do, we believe we are not doing enough; we then throw ourselves back into trying to make things happen. Whenever we are bouncing between these two extremes, we end up getting nowhere because it's impossible to really gain any momentum. So which is a "better" approach: being extremely proactive or allowing things to happen naturally? The answer is neither.

Does surrendering mean we hand *everything* over to a Higher Power and just sit around waiting for destiny to knock at our door? No! As we are spiritual beings having a human experience, surrender is often a process of letting things happen naturally while being attuned to the feedback we are getting from the Universe. I call this "proactive surrender." Proactive surrender is very different from either resignation or control: it does not mean giving up and doing nothing at all, nor does it mean fighting against reality, attempting to force things to happen.

Shortly after my thirty-fifth birthday, when I went in for my yearly gyne-cological exam, my doctor shared the disappointing news that my fertility was declining. This was like a punch in the gut. My doctor reminded me of the option to freeze my eggs, and at first, I was against it. There were the practical reasons like the large expense, the physical and emotional discomfort, and the risks involved. And there were the more spiritual reasons that had to do with my belief systems: if God wants me to have a child, it's really up to Him.

To make sure I was not just resigning and calling it surrender, I stepped into proactive surrender, which involved going within and then asking for external feedback. I meditated, asked for help, and enlisted the assistance of the Seeker to be observant of any guidance I was receiving. Within the next week, three significant things happened. First, a friend announced I must meet a friend of hers. So we set a lunch date, and within the first fifteen min-utes, the conversation led to her choice to freeze her eggs and how liberating it was for her. Second, while on the road, I went to work out at a hotel gym, where the TV was on, and there just happened to be a news report on the new advances in egg freezing. Third, I was sitting at a restaurant, waiting for a friend, and overheard the conversation of the two women sitting next to me. One of the women was talking about problems she was having with fertility and said, "I just wish I had frozen my eggs when I was younger." Clearly, my prayer had been answered.

I learned that surrender does not mean just letting go of a dream entirely, but rather being open to how something will happen, while taking value-aligned action steps in support of the dream. Spirit meets us at our point of action and intention.

The decision to freeze my eggs felt both like a value-aligned action and a way to surrender to the "what is" of my life. The truth was that I did want kids, and I surrendered to the fact that, for whatever reason, there was not a man in my life to have them with yet. I felt empowered by proactive surren-der and also began to look for all the ways I do express the essence of being a mother right now with my clients, friends, and readers. And I'm happy to report that I now have a total of eleven viable eggs frozen.

Here is a prayer you can use to help yourself practice proactive surrender: "God, please help me to know what my next step is and to recognize it when you put it before me. Grant me the courage and willingness to take it. Bless me with the knowledge that everything happens in perfect Divine time."

TRANSFORMATIONAL TRUTH
Things Happen in Due Time

A common complaint from individuals dealing with disappointment is "I am doing all this work on myself, and I feel different inside. But things in my life are not changing." They've followed the Expectation Hangover treatment plan perfectly, so where is the money, job, health, or relationship? If you feel that your external world is not reflective of the "new you," please do not get discouraged by interpreting it as feedback that you aren't doing enough.

The truth is that physical reality (the goal line) is very dense, unlike our emotional, mental, or spiritual world (the soul line), where change is more fluid and immediate.

> "The value of not getting what I want when I want it has taught me that everything is Divine timing. No matter how much I want things or situations to move faster, everything happens when it's meant to be. I find peace when I trust that God knows what's best for us, when things need to happen in our life, and, most important, when we are ready for it. Although sometimes we feel we are ready for things in life, sometimes we are truly not."
> — Abira

Interesting little fact: a bamboo seed takes up to seven years to sprout, but once it does, it can grow thirteen feet in only one week. Unbelievable! Sometimes the seeds we plant do take time to sprout. The growth work we do requires a gestation period, and things happen in due time. We must give up our desire for instant gratification and our obsession with results, and measure progress by the differences felt inside rather than by what is different on the outside. It is normal to feel like big dreams are taking forever to come true, to wonder if you are doing something wrong, and to think perhaps you should settle for less. But I assure you that no matter how long it takes, once it happens, you will wonder how you ever doubted it and be glad you never settled.

LESSON QUEST

"We have all a better guide in ourselves, if we would attend to it,
than any other person can be."
— Jane Austen

I promised you at the beginning of this book that I would not say that everything happens for a reason without sharing with you how to discover the reason. Now it is time for that discovery. You are about to embark on a journey on the soul line by answering the question "What is my soul seeking to help me learn through my Expectation Hangover?" This journey will demand that you take "response-ability" for your life — not in the sense of blaming yourself, but in the sense that you have the *ability* to *respond* to the situations in your life from the position of a Seeker rather than a victim. This quest will take you to new heights where you will have the spiritual altitude to see the events in your life from an elevated perspective. On this quest, you will experience many miracles as you change your perceptions. As a Seeker, you travel light and know that judgment is a heavy load to carry. You are equipped with a headlamp that shines light during the dark times. This lamp represents your insight. Notice that word: *in-sight*. This is a quest you will take alone, as spiritual wisdom comes from getting quiet, being still, and going within. No one can answer your deepest questions but you.

"What my Expectation Hangover taught me is that it all happened for a reason. Because of my dysfunctional upbringing, I did not do too well in high school or finish college, but my experiences made me who I am today. The 'street smarts' I have, the spiritual enlightenment, the way I process emotions and things in my daily life cannot be taught in any school. I understand the big picture, the Higher Power that guides me daily, and I could not be more grateful. The person I am today came from the struggles I had all my yesterdays and affects who I am growing into tomorrow."
— Sagen

A caution for your quest: do not expect to "figure out" all the lessons of your Expectation Hangover. Some will come quickly in the form of great epiphanies, and some will reveal themselves to you slowly over time. Through your awakened faith, you will see that what is dark right now will one day become light and that what you do not know will be shown to you in time. Have patience with yourself, your process, and Divine timing.

Although I felt I'd overcome the disappointment of my fiancé breaking up with me in my twenties, the biggest soul lesson did not reveal itself to me until very recently (nearly ten years later). I rarely thought about my ex-fiancé, and I felt a sense of completion with that relationship; but there was one gem I had not yet gathered from that particular Expectation Hangover. And because Spirit is such a marvelous and thorough teacher, during a meditation, I unexpectedly got the lesson I missed. I received the insight, but not until I was ready for it.

My client Adam helped build a company but ended up leaving with a massive Expectation Hangover after his partners forced him out. Recently, he found out the company sold for thirty million dollars. Had he stood up to his partners and stayed, he would have received half of that money. He told me about this with a huge smile on his face as he shared how he was not upset at all over not getting any of the money: "Sure, the money would have been nice, but without the experience of being unfairly forced out of that company, I would not be the man, the father, the husband, the creative entrepreneur, and the seeker I am today. The disappointment from that exit put me on my spiritual path — and that is priceless."

Again, you do not have control over what happens in life, but you do have dominion over how you respond to it. At the University of Santa Monica, we say, "How you relate to the issue is the issue." Are you ready to relate to the issue of your Expectation Hangover as a Seeker and tap into your resourcefulness? As you do so, you will strengthen the muscles of your inner Seeker so that you will default to valuing the opportunities and blessings in every Expectation Hangover more than any external outcome. When we connect the dots in our lives, we gain clarity. Those "aha moments" in life open up space in our mind that was previously crowded with misunderstanding.

> "Bad times have a scientific value.
> These are occasions a good learner would not miss."
> — Ralph Waldo Emerson

❋ **EXERCISE**
Exploring Your Spiritual Curriculum

Begin by centering yourself in the present moment and connecting to the Seeker. Set an intention to move through this exercise with a judgment-free approach. Be a miracle maker in your own life by being willing to see your Expectation Hangovers from a different perspective. When you feel attuned to the Seeker, respond to the following questions in your journal, focusing on one of your Expectation Hangovers.

1. What external goal-line attachments is your Expectation Hangover giving you the opportunity to release?
2. What changes is your Expectation Hangover giving you the opportunity to make?
3. How are your challenges actually serving you rather than punishing you?
4. In what way is your Expectation Hangover catalyzing a different relationship with yourself? In what way is it catalyzing a relationship with Spirit?
5. What about your Expectation Hangover are you grateful for?
6. From the Seeker's perspective, given your responses to questions 1–5, what are the major lessons of your life curriculum?

Complete this exercise for as many Expectation Hangovers as you like. Be a thorough Seeker! The more Expectation Hangovers you explore, the more advanced an understanding you will have of your life curriculum.

. . . .

NORA'S STORY

I was completely broke and filled with self-judgment about my dismal financial situation. I started aggressively looking for a higher-paying job. I thought that all my problems would be solved when I was flown across North America to be wined and dined at the headquarters of a rapidly growing software company. When I accepted the position, my salary more than doubled. I thought I had finally made it — I had achieved career success! The months that followed were devastatingly disappointing. Sure, my paychecks were bigger, but I was also working double the hours at triple the pace. I was micromanaged to the minute; the company culture was shallow and cutthroat; and the work itself was tedious and boring. The travel schedule was so rigorous that I had to spend my vacation time catching up on sleep and errands. The more my bank account grew, the angrier I became that I did not have time to spend the money. At the height of my Expectation Hangover, I was confused, beyond stressed-out, and beginning to realize my formula for success was failing.

So I quit and leaped into the unknown. I began seeking out what got me into this situation in the first place. The biggest lesson I learned is that I had been letting my net worth define my self-worth. For most of my life, I bought into the belief that once I made a lot of money, I'd feel good about myself. I see now that I had to have the experience of making a lot of money but still being miserable, to learn how to untangle my sense of self-worth from my salary. Once I got clear on what I wanted my life to look like, I was able to see that the resource I really needed more of was time, not money.

Experiencing both a low-paying job and a workaholic culture taught me to appreciate both time and money when I have them, because both can be scarce. I learned to manage my money and do more with less. I gained clarity on what is important to me in a job, courage when it comes to making my own rules, and insight on how to be discerning. I was able to walk away from offers of a high salary in favor of work-life balance and not judge myself as unsuccessful. Eventually, I did find a job that allowed me to work a forty-hour workweek, and that is when my goals outside of work really took off. I completed a yoga teacher training course, traveled to Costa Rica, learned how to surf, decorated my apartment, read voraciously, and took up backcountry skiing. Even though my bank account was not as shiny, my soul was delighted.

YOUR LIFE PURPOSE

Nearly every person I have encountered is, or has at some point been, searching for their life purpose — usually in the form of a career, person, or family. But the true, and really the *only*, purpose of life is to grow and become more aware of the Love we are, and then share that Love in the form of relationships, self-expression, and work.

Last year I met a forty-year-old man who had lived between Costa Rica and the United States for many years but now lives full-time in Costa Rica. When I asked him why, he said, "Because Americans don't understand what the purpose of life is." "We don't? Well, what is it?" I asked. He smiled at me with the kind of smile someone gives you when they have an incredible insight they are about to share, and said, "The purpose of life is to *love*. Here we know that. And we are happy. There everyone is looking for something or someone to be their purpose rather than enjoying every moment and living life. I live my life, every moment of it, and that is my purpose."

Now, I wish that an insight from a man in Costa Rica would be all you needed to hear to let go of your desire to find something that feels purposeful, but I know it's not. My guess is you are probably not going to move to Costa Rica tomorrow, drink from coconuts, and bask in the Love that you are. I understand you would really love to *do* things you love and feel purposeful.

A piece of advice we often hear when it comes to discovering our purpose in life is to "follow our passion." But before you can follow your passion, you have to find it. So where do you look for it? How do you discover what you are deeply passionate about from the perspective of the soul line rather than the goal line?

You may have sought out clues to your passion in things like personality inventories, self-help books, or career assessment tests. Or perhaps you are considering your hobbies or looking back to things you enjoyed as a kid to gather some clues about what you love. Although those places may offer you great insight, I encourage you to look for your passion somewhere else: in your Expectation Hangovers.

Did you know that the original definition of the word *passion* was actually "suffering"? (It referred to the sufferings of Jesus between the night of the Last Supper and his death.) Over time the word *passion* has evolved to mean "love; a strong liking or desire for or devotion to some activity, object, or concept." So the word means two things: suffering and love. There is key information in this.

Most people I know who are doing something they are truly passionate about were inspired by their Expectation Hangovers, myself included!

Akirah finally found the courage to end an abusive relationship with the man she had planned on marrying. Initially, she was depressed and jealous of friends in healthy relationships. She withdrew from people and turned to drinking and dating to escape her pain. She eventually allowed herself to grieve and joined a support group for survivors of domestic abuse. Today she is passionate about teaching women and girls about abuse and healthy relationships. She says:

> I'm now married to a wonderful man, but had I never experienced abuse, I would have never identified my passion for sharing my story. I want to teach women and girls about abuse and the importance of pursuing healthy relationships. I firmly believe I was put on the planet to spread awareness of this issue. Through writing and speaking, I see the connections I form with awesome ladies from all over as the biggest blessings of all. In honor of those whose lives were taken by an abusive partner, I take this work very seriously. It is the best thing that has ever happened to me. It is my blessing from God and my offering to others.

I encourage you to put away the personality tests, books, and advice from others for a moment and examine your own life curriculum to discover the key to your passion. Your passion is within you. It is not something you need to seek outside yourself. Just as the word *passion* evolved from "suffering" to "love," see how you can evolve and awaken that passion inside of you by viewing your Expectation Hangover from the altitude of a Seeker. When you truly understand that *everything* that has happened in your life has been for your Highest Good, you will naturally be called to serve rather than experiencing any suffering.

As we clear out our disappointment, the impulse is to share all the love we have rediscovered and lessons we have learned. This service does not necessarily need to translate to a career. You don't have to be a speaker, write a book, coach, start a business, set up a nonprofit organization, or have a platform of any kind to contribute. You share your lessons and blessings with all the people you interact with, from your spouse to the clerk at the grocery store. You express them in any kind of work you do, whether you like your job or not. You live your calling by the unique ways that you express yourself and touch the planet. True passion is love — loving who we are, loving what we do, loving each other, and sharing love wherever we go.

"Work is love made visible."
— Kahlil Gibran

✳ **EXERCISE**
Downloading Your Purpose

Spend some time reflecting on what your greatest Expectation Hangovers (as a source of suffering in your life) have been, then respond to the following questions in your journal.

1. What have been the challenges? What are the unique things you have gone through? (Whatever you've gone through is important — do not minimize anything!)

2. Have you experienced certain patterns in your suffering, such as feeling abandoned, unworthy, or isolated?

3. What insights have you gathered from your suffering when you've looked at it from an empowered rather than a victim perspective — when you've looked at it without judgment or thinking any of it was wrong?

4. What actions (inner and outer) have you taken to heal your suffering and move into compassion and forgiveness?

5. If you were speaking with someone you care for deeply who was experiencing a similar Expectation Hangover, what advice would you offer?

6. What is the change you so deeply want to see in the world?

• • • •

Have deep reverence for all the Expectation Hangovers you have endured in life. It has all been in service to your learning and the legacy you are here to leave. Love it *all* and I assure you that you will find your passion.

MARCIA'S STORY

When I was twenty-seven, I was diagnosed with stage-three ovarian cancer. I was newly married and ready to start a family. My expectation was to get pregnant and have my child that year. Instead, a surgery was scheduled to remove the tumor, and the doctor assured me I could have children, even with one ovary remaining. I was expected to recover quickly and be back to work in a week. The Expectation Hangover got even worse after the doctors opened me up in surgery and found cancer spread throughout my abdomen. An emergency hysterectomy was necessary. When I woke up, the doctor broke the news. I was devastated by the cancer and unexpected infertility.

My husband and I struggled through the treatment process and dealing with infertility. We divorced one year to the day from the date of my diagnosis. I had to move cross-country and back in with my parents. I dealt with my grief through counseling. I spent a short time feeling like a victim; but then I realized how much more suffering being a victim actually created, and I decided to take a different approach. Fear told me that I would never recover, but faith told me that there was a reason I was going through this. I listened to faith instead of fear and began to ask, "What am I learning?"

The answer was that this seemingly devastating Expectation Hangover was truly the beginning of a whole life that looked nothing like the life I expected. The cancer and divorce catapulted me to levels of compassion and love for myself that I had never experienced. Even with a piece of me missing, I felt more complete than ever. Five years after my divorce, I met my current husband. We just celebrated our tenth anniversary and have seven-year-old twin boys thanks to the help of a surrogate and egg donor.

A few years later, more of the "reason" for my Expectation Hangover was revealed. I felt a huge call to help other families after a cancer diagnosis so they too could see it as a new beginning rather than a death sentence. With the help of our surrogate and other friends, I started a nonprofit, which is an online support forum that allows patients and caregivers to easily connect with family and friends. We make sure no one goes through cancer alone.

✧ **TOOL**
   Prayer

"Never forget the three powerful resources you always have available to you:
love, prayer, and forgiveness."
— H. Jackson Brown Jr.

Prayer is another powerful practice to engage in to grow on the soul line and treat your Expectation Hangover. I've seen many people who question religious structures discount the effectiveness of prayer, but this is like throwing the baby out with the holy water!

Prayer is a bit different from meditation in that prayer involves actively invoking or speaking to Spirit, whereas meditation is a process of being still and receptive. I like to think of prayer as having a little talk with Spirit, in the same way I'd open up to a trusted friend. You do not have to know what you are going to say; just open your heart and begin the conversation. Simply take a moment to center yourself by bringing your attention to your breath, then take three deep, slow breaths into your heart space and just begin. I find it helpful to pray out loud so my mind does not wander and so I am more fully anchored in the energy of prayer. Trust that there is no wrong way to pray (except not doing it!).

Adjusting what you are praying for will profoundly shift your experience of prayer. A lot of us tend to think of Spirit as a waiter. We place our order with the Universe and expect it will come back to us just the way we like it. Or we think of Spirit as a judge we negotiate with — "If you do this for me, then I will do this." If our prayers are not answered in the way we expected, not only are we faced with an Expectation Hangover, but we also begin to question our faith. Praying for "my will" versus "thy will" leads to missing out on the opportunity to step into greater faith.

Instead of asking for some outcome or negotiating with Spirit, pray for what you would like to experience. For example, during the time after my divorce, when being single was so disappointing for me, I shifted the way I prayed. Instead of asking for a man to come into my life, I prayed for Spirit to help me alleviate my suffering over my relationship status. I prayed for grace and asked for a great experience of feeling connected to Spirit. I asked for Spirit to help me remember I was not alone.

If your prayer is focused on asking for help with dropping your judgments and moving into acceptance, rather than on asking for specific results, you just might find your prayers are answered a lot more often. Stop praying for material things and start praying for the internal experiences you would like to cultivate during your Expectation Hangover, like deeper levels of understanding, connection, grace, and healing. That way, you are asking for Spirit's assistance in dealing with the reality of your life rather than praying for it to be different. Every prayer is answered; sometimes the answer is "no" or "not yet." Rejection is often protection. Have faith that Spirit has a *better* idea in store.

Here are a few of my favorite prayers:

> "Spirit, help me see myself the way you see me. And help me see others the way you see me."
>
> "I am willing to see the lessons in this situation. Show me the way."
>
> "Use me as your instrument."
>
> "Thy will be done."
>
> And perhaps the most powerful prayer of all: "Thank you."

All that said, I still like to share my preferences with Spirit. What I mean by this is that in my prayer, I will speak my desires and longings, but without any attachment or requests. I do this by always asking for "this or something better, for the Highest Good of all concerned."

Prayer is a wonderful way to ask for support, but don't forget to also ask your fellow classmates. Rely on your Higher Power, but do not make that the only thing you lean on. Reach out to loved ones and support groups to assist you and remind you that you are connected not just to a Higher Power, but to other loving souls as well.

Cher's Expectation Hangover started when she moved her family from Arizona to California, a move she thought would be a regular transition. The move took an enormous financial and emotional toll; she lost a friend to cancer; her dog died; and her husband got very sick. "My life started to feel like a country western song," she says. "Every bad thing that could happen, did!" By reaching out for support, breaking patterns of isolating herself during difficult times, and praying, Cher is now on the other side of her Expectation Hangover. As she explains it: "Tragedy can hit home just like that. I started to pray not for bad things not to happen, but to have the strength for whatever does happen that might be tough to handle. That change in prayer helped me to get out of thinking about when the next shoe was going to drop and to believe that I could handle anything that life threw my way."

· · · ·

TRANSFORMATIONAL TRUTH
Leaps of Faith Come with Free Falls

"You have to take risks. We will only understand the miracle of life fully when we allow the unexpected to happen."
— Paulo Coelho

Leaps of faith are alluring because we are leaping out of something that isn't in alignment with our desires; however, when we are standing on the edge of a cliff facing uncertainty, it suddenly becomes petrifying. We hear inspirational stories of people who took great leaps of faith and (by the time we hear their story) landed somewhere with greater passion, purpose, and prosperity. This makes a great advertisement for leaping into the unknown but doesn't tell the whole story. You may have expected that once you leaped, a fluffy white cloud would be there to catch you or you'd land softly on a beautiful ledge full of everything you want. If that happened, fantastic! But chances are you are in the unadvertised and rather scary part of taking a leap of faith: the free fall.

Every leap of faith comes with a free-fall period — expect it. The free fall can last for days, months, even years. Your ego will begin to panic and search for some kind of certainty to grab on to. A lot of fear may come up, and you may even question your choice to take the leap. So how can you avoid falling right into an Expectation Hangover?

First, know that a free-fall period is the time when faith is developed. Faith is not developed in times of certainty, but rather in the vast sea of the unknown. Many people confuse having faith with being right. For instance, if you take a leap of faith and everything goes according to your plan or dream, you think, "Whew, I was really right about taking that leap." That is not faith; it is simply your ego feeling proud of itself. Faith is not based on results. Faith is being able to be totally at peace with what is and trusting the Universe even if the white cloud or ledge isn't in sight.

Second, don't look down. If you have ever been somewhere really high up, you probably felt a lot calmer if you didn't look down. Imagining worst-case scenarios during a free fall is like looking down. A free fall is scary enough because you are spiraling through uncertainty; don't make it worse with a lot of what-ifs followed by negative statements.

Finally, don't look behind you. Regret is pointless. You made the choice and took the leap. Trust yourself. There is no turning back, and that is good news. Stay present. Look at what's in front of you.

In order for any change to occur, there is a period of chaos. Chaos isn't bad; it means things are changing. Taking a leap is a powerful action step out of disappointment. Even if you're apprehensive, go for it. A free fall can be a beautiful time of expectation-free surrender. Stop questioning. Start accepting what is. Start enjoying the excitement of uncertainty. Start trusting. And start today. Take a leap of faith.

CONCLUSION

It is up to each one of us to change the world through the changes we make within ourselves. Each judgment that we forgive and each Expectation Hangover that we reframe as a loving, necessary lesson in our spiritual curriculum elevates our consciousness. We are all connected, so as we heal and transform, we are contributing to healing the planet. Imagine the *profound* impact your love has on the world. You do make a difference. By simply embodying light and love, you become a miracle worker. As you process your part of the pain, self-doubt, limiting beliefs, and separation that we all suffer as part of the human experience, you elevate the consciousness of the collective. Do not underestimate the power of your personal transformation freed of judgment. Moving forward with a learning-oriented approach to life, you awaken to true compassion and service. You are a Seeker. And you are absolutely Divine.

> "As we become spiritually mature, we attune to our Soul nature.
> We participate. We see that the world is the screen upon which we
> project ourselves, so if we see flaws out there, we are the ones who need
> to change. And this change can only take place by discovering
> our true nature, the Divine within us."
> — John-Roger

Part Three

PREVENTION

Chapter Ten

MANAGING YOUR EXPECTATIONS

"My happiness grows in direct proportion to my acceptance, and in inverse proportion to my expectations."

— Michael J. Fox

If you have walked through the doorway of transformation and celebrated the lessons learned from your Expectation Hangover, does that mean you will never be disappointed again? Most likely the answer is no. What it does mean is that you are now well equipped to decrease both the frequency of future Expectation Hangovers and the amount of time you spend in disappointment when they hit.

The treatment plan you learned in part 2 now becomes part of your prevention plan. Use role-playing Rx and the tools you learned to decrease the duration of any Expectation Hangover you face. Growth is a process, not an event. You can't upgrade yourself the way you do your iPhone. If you find yourself slipping into old habits, reactions, or choices that you thought were behind you, that does not mean change is not occurring. You may take ten steps forward and then eight steps back. But the next time, you will take eleven steps forward and only seven steps back. The more you use your treatment plan, the less time you will spend in disappointment. Whatever you do, just keep going. The following illustration shows the way we sometimes think growth and personal development should occur and the way they really happen:

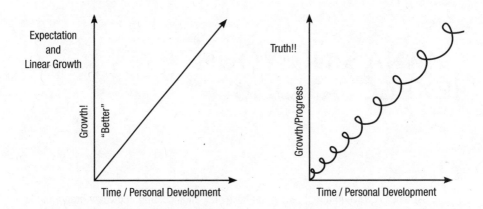

Your prevention plan is not about keeping Expectation Hangovers from ever happening again. If I promised you that, I'd be setting you up for another one. It is not realistic to expect to never be disappointed again — you are human, after all!

You can, however, manage your expectations. If you have unrealistic expectations, you will be disappointed more frequently. You have learned that you do not have complete control over everything that happens in your life and that nothing outside of you will fulfill you. Remember that we grow through struggle, so just when you settle into your comfort zone, unexpected disruption may be around the corner. Keep in mind that everyone else is working through their own curriculum and will do things that you may find upsetting. Manage your expectations by becoming more and more aware of when you are falling into the illusion of control or when/then thinking and when you are expecting too much.

"Adjusting my expectations of what a relationship can provide for me, and becoming more aware of how much I can actually provide for myself, have been key to avoiding disappointment. I no longer expect a romantic relationship to solve all my problems and make me feel whole. I accept much more accountability for my own happiness, and I am much more proactive about taking care of my own needs."
— Dorothea

Please do not confuse having realistic expectations with lowering your standards, settling for "average," accepting poor performance, or letting people walk all over you. Just make room for the variety of life, which includes bad days, bad moods, and unexpected curveballs.

> "Life doesn't always go as planned. One of the best ways to deal
> with this inevitability is to stop expecting it to be otherwise.
> So ease off your expectations a little and see how much nicer your life can be."
> — Richard Carlson

THE SECRET SAUCE FOR PURSUING GOALS

A client recently sent the following question to me after spending about a month treating her Expectation Hangover: "All right, I get that it's not great for me to have expectations, but there are things that I want in life. I have dreams and desires. How do I pursue them and not set myself up for an Expectation Hangover? Am I not supposed to want things or have goals?" The answer lies in knowing the recipe to the secret sauce for pursuing goals without setting ourselves up for an Expectation Hangover.

There are four ways to pursue goals:

- With low involvement and low attachment
- With low involvement and high attachment
- With high involvement and high attachment
- With high involvement and low attachment

Involvement is the degree to which we proactively participate in the pursuit of our goals. Attachment is the degree to which our well-being, sense of worthiness, happiness, and peace of mind are dependent on reaching our goals. We create attachment whenever we become invested in a desired outcome, plan, or opinion. When we have any degree of attachment, we have expectations. And when we have expectations, we can have — you guessed it — Expectation Hangovers.

A low involvement–low attachment approach means that we have a goal but are not doing much to make it happen, and it really is not something we are very emotionally invested in. In this scenario, we typically think we should do something but have a "why bother" approach and end up taking minimal steps, if any, toward our goal. Steve consistently felt he should work out but only went to the gym once a week. He was fairly apathetic about getting in shape, which resulted in an Expectation Hangover about letting himself down and not losing weight.

A low involvement–high attachment approach means we really, really want something to happen, and think life would be much better if we had it, but are not actively taking steps toward it. In both low involvement–low attachment and low involvement–high attachment, you see the world as happening *to* you and remain a victim of your circumstances. Lindsey believed that once she was in a relationship, she would break free of her romantic rut and low self-confidence, yet she refused to put herself on any online dating sites or pursue coaching on relationships. Her inaction resulted in an Expectation Hangover about not being married at the age she anticipated.

A high involvement–high attachment approach means we are passionate about a goal and actively taking steps to make it happen. We are very attached to the outcome, believing that once we attain it, we will experience something we are longing for. With this approach, you see the world as happening *by* you, and you believe you can control outcomes with enough effort. So you experience a sense of failure if an outcome fails to materialize. It is a level of overresponsibility that becomes exhausting, and potentially even devastating. Katrina was convinced she was supposed to be a famous actress. She took acting classes, went to auditions, and created poster boards with ideal scenes about her career. Being an actress mattered so much to her that every time she did not land a part, she had a painful Expectation Hangover that made her feel rejected and worthless. Katrina was only happy and confident when she got an acting part.

That leaves us with pursuing goals with high involvement and low attachment — the best recipe for going after what you want without setting yourself up for an Expectation Hangover. In this approach, you have a strong intention to cocreate (together with the Universe) things in your life that are in alignment with your values and goals, but you are not attached to the outcome. Your sense of worthiness, success, or happiness is not tied to whether or not particular things happen. And you remain open to things manifesting in forms different than you may have expected. By practicing high involvement–low attachment, you move into a perspective where you see things happening *through* you and surrender control, understanding that you are a cocreator with the Universe. You recognize that effort and commitment are important but that results are not completely up to you and do not dictate your overall well-being.

Tony's experience illustrates high involvement–low attachment. He was inspired to start his own business. He hired me as a coach, enrolled in several business and entrepreneurial courses, moved to a less expensive apartment, and created a detailed business plan. He remained focused on his vision but in the meantime continued to find his happiness and worth inside himself. When he launched his first product and did not hit the expected numbers, Tony practiced nonattachment by not taking it personally or taking it to mean he had failed. Although he felt some disappointment, he was not devastated. He used Horseback Rider Rx to reframe it as a learning experience. He called upon the Scientist, to respond more proactively, which moved him toward his core values of confidence and courage.

Use the secret sauce of high involvement–low attachment so you live in "through me" consciousness. Wanting things is not wrong. You are worthy and deserving of your dreams. What sets you up for disappointment is not your desires, but your attachment to your expectations.

ADITI'S STORY

After getting to the other side of an Expectation Hangover about being laid off, I did my part in applying for jobs and preparing and showing up for interviews. But when I was not being hired, I began to see that perhaps I was not meant to go back to my previous field of work. Instead of being completely attached to finding a new job, I started doing things I truly enjoy and began paying more attention to where I was being led. Rather than fill up my entire calendar, I consciously created space and said yes to invitations I would have passed up in the past, like going to a zumba class! I found myself taking great interest in holistic health. I had never considered going into health coaching on my own; but the idea came to me, and I found some interested clients. I found that I made sure to continue taking action steps, but if things weren't happening the way I hoped, I saw that life was perhaps taking me in a different direction. The more I was open to being led, the more synchronicity occurred.

Chapter Eleven

QUICK FIXES THAT WORK

"It's not whether you get knocked down, it's whether you get up."
— Vince Lombardi

Up to now I have cautioned against quick fixes. However, there *are* things you can do that not only offer instant relief from Expectation Hangovers, but also prevent them from happening in the first place. You may be wondering, "Jeez, why didn't you just tell me this in the first chapter?" Because you had to milk your disappointment first! Now that you've journeyed through your treatment plan and cleared out emotional clutter, rewired your mind, altered your behavior, and grown in consciousness, these quick fixes will actually work.

QUICK FIX 1: STOP PEOPLE-PLEASING

"Your time is limited, so don't waste it living someone else's life....
Don't let the noise of others' opinions drown out your own inner voice.
And most important, have the courage to follow your heart and intuition."
— Steve Jobs

It is natural to want to fit in and not upset others, because it feels safer. The feeling of letting people down and perhaps contributing to their Expectation Hangovers is one we would rather avoid. All it takes is one small experience of feeling criticized or not liked, thinking we've upset someone, or getting tons of praise and validation for making others happy to develop people pleasing as a habit. We think that pleasing others prevents Expectation Hangovers, but it actually sets us up for more because we put the opinions and expectations of others above our own, making our self-worth and choices reliant on an external source.

"I gave myself permission to be normal and happy despite what others think. I always remember to focus instead on what I expect of me, which is to put my God-given talents to good use. As long as I'm proud of myself, that's what matters, and that's how I sleep well at night."

— Jeannie

People pleasing depletes your most valuable resources: time and energy. Just think how much energy you waste by obsessing about what other people think of you or strategizing your actions to appease others. I am all for being a considerate and generous person. And it feels wonderful to love others! But being and acting from love is *not* people pleasing. People pleasing is different because it involves an attachment to someone else's reaction. And as you've learned, when there is attachment, there is a high risk of an Expectation Hangover.

You may think being a people pleaser makes you a "good" person, but I am going to offer you a radical reframe of people pleasing: it's selfish to be a people pleaser. Why? Because being attached to pleasing others is really about you. You want to be liked. You do not want to upset anyone. You want to look good for others. You are protecting yourself from confrontation. Furthermore, you are the one who is choosing to withhold expressing who you *truly* are. And by doing all those things, you are keeping yourself, your light, and your love from the world — and that is selfish.

Stop being selfish and be self-honoring instead, by making choices that support your core values. Making choices based on how you will be perceived by others, how someone else will respond, or what you think you should do may violate your values. A self-honoring choice is not selfish. You can be for yourself without being against anyone else. Selfish people usually aren't concerned about whether their choices are selfish because they are too self-absorbed or self-centered to consider it. Just the fact that you are questioning being selfish is an indicator that you aren't.

How people respond is their responsibility, not yours! I know this may sound crazy to you, but we really do not have the power to *make* anyone feel anything. You are only responsible for honestly communicating without going into blame, finger-pointing, ultimatums, or expectations.

Often the self-honoring choice is choosing not to make a decision. Just because a choice is put in front of you doesn't mean you have to choose instantly. It's self-honoring to say "I don't know," or "I need time to think about that," or "Let me get back to you." And often the most self-honoring choice is to say "No." That's a complete sentence. It's not necessary to follow "No" with a justification or apology. You are not obligated to explain yourself. It's enough to just say "No" if that's your truth.

"I have spent most of my life being the good girl and living up to society's expectations, and it hasn't brought me the happiness I want. It's easier said than done, but now I am starting to ask myself what I want and not what other people think I should be or do."

— Casey

I encourage you to take a big step today toward preventing future Expectation Hangovers by filling in the blanks to this statement: "If I let go of caring what…think(s), I would…" I understand it may be scary, but what's even scarier is making choices that violate your values, because it builds resentment. Your value does not come from the way others perceive you. Your life is not defined by the expectations of others. What other people think of you is none of your business.

QUICK FIX 2: GO YOUR OWN WAY

Your intuition is your inner compass, and it will always steer you in a direction that is most aligned with your superpowers and core values. Often directives from our intuition seem random, but do not let that stop you from responding. Our mind likes to know the entire grand plan for life, while our intuition guides us one moment at a time, leading us to experiences, rather than outcomes, that feed our soul and plant the seeds of our next steps.

Last March in my morning meditation, I kept hearing "Australia, Australia, Australia." Australia wasn't on my mind at all, but I've learned that messages from my intuition tend to not make logical sense; my antenna was up. Shortly thereafter I got two new clients from Australia, received several emails from people in the Sydney area about whether or not I would go there to teach, and randomly turned on NPR one morning in the middle of a story about...Australia!

"Hmmm," I thought, "what if I am supposed to go teach there?" Then all kinds of questions from my logical mind came up: When do I go? How do I plan an event in another country? How will I market it? These questions only stopped me. Then my intuition nudged me again as I heard "Book a ticket." So I did. I bought a ticket without any clue why I was going. At the very least, I thought, I'd have a vacation. Then a series of synchronicities happened. People dropped into my life to support *all* the logistics, PR, staffing, and marketing of my event. Wonderful new Australian friends offered to host me. I had places to stay, got an upgrade to business class, *and* happened to go during the best time of year. All because I listened to my intuition.

Your intuition will not lead you to an Expectation Hangover — you just need to allow it to lead. Everyone has intuition. Yes, even you! But our intuition is not pushy and loud like our logical minds. It is more often a whisper than a shout, so set aside time to meditate and get quiet enough to hear. Perhaps there is an incredible insight waiting, but your mind is so distracted by anxiety, fear, or attachment to your comfort zone that your Higher Self is having a hard time getting through to you.

Stop attempting to "figure out" things with your logical mind. Stop running to others for answers to questions about your life. Stop waiting for some kind of lighting-bolt sign and pay more attention to the subtleties. Start listening to *yourself* and go your own way.

QUICK FIX 3: DON'T GO TO A CHINESE RESTAURANT FOR NACHOS

"When you stop expecting people to be perfect,
you can like them for who they are."
— Donald Miller

If you were craving nachos, would you go to a Chinese restaurant? No! Because you know that in a Chinese restaurant, they don't serve nachos. In fact, they probably wouldn't even have the ingredients to make them. If you really wanted nachos, you would go somewhere where they serve them, right? Now think about who you go to when you are craving support, encouragement, guidance, unbiased advice, loving feedback, or acknowledgment. Do you go to people who are consistently able to dish out what you are hungry for? Or do you find yourself going to people who do not have what you need on their menu and then find yourself consistently discouraged and disappointed?

Most of the time, we know what we are craving when we reach out to someone else. If someone in your life has consistently reacted and responded in a way that has not satisfied your needs, chances are they do not have the ingredients to do so. Continuing to go to that person, hoping that someday what you are hungry for appears on their menu, is like continuing to walk into a Chinese restaurant when you want nachos. You may get fed, but not with what you truly wanted to eat. And now the only leftover you have is an Expectation Hangover.

Beth had a perpetual Expectation Hangover regarding her father. She always had a dream that he would be involved in the life of his grandchildren, especially once he retired. Despite her attempts to have him play a bigger role by consistently inviting him to gatherings, sending pictures, and dropping by to spend time with him, he would either not show up or not be engaged if he was there. Although, as a father, he had been absent and disengaged, Beth was expecting him to be a different kind of grandfather. Beth explains:

> As soon as I let go of the fantasy of who I wanted him to be and accepted him for who he was, I was no longer disappointed. Because I was so invested in changing my dad, I lost sight of how amazing a father my husband is. Now not only am I free of my Expectation Hangover; I am even more aware of the blessings in my life because I am focused on what I have rather than what is missing.

We cannot change people. I repeat: *we cannot change people*. This can be especially challenging when you really want a significant person in your life, such as a parent or romantic partner, to be able to satisfy your cravings. However, sometimes they just don't have the ingredients to do so. Other people are not wrong if they don't live up to your expectations; they are who they are. Accept what they do have to offer you.

Think of some of your common "cravings" that involve being supported by others: someone to just listen; an objective resource for feedback; someone to laugh with; someone you feel safe to be vulnerable with; a person who will offer time and physical assistance when you need help with a move or project; or someone who is encouraging. Now consider which people you go to for those things but who you come away from with an Expectation Hangover. Make a commitment to yourself that you will stop going to them when you have a craving for something they cannot dish out. Love and accept them for who they are; they are doing the best they can. Consider the people who do match up with some of your cravings — there may be a lot of cooks in your kitchen that you might not have been aware of because you were hanging on to expectations of others. Being conscious and proactive regarding our expectations of others is how we get desires and needs met in healthy and expectation-free ways.

It is true that we can be catalysts for another person's change, but in most cases in order to be that catalyst, we have to be totally unattached to being it. Working and endlessly hoping to change someone else will not only lead to an Expectation Hangover, but it will also distract you from doing your own work. Often it is detachment, acceptance, and honoring our own truth that inspire others to find the truth within themselves.

QUICK FIX 4: WAKE UP FROM COMPARISON COMAS

"The key to being strong is to stop comparing. Don't compare your body, job, life, or experience with others because everyone is coming from different experiences and angles, and we're all exactly where we need to be. Let go of your story, because that's all it is — be yourself completely as you are."
— Kathryn Budig

Comparing ourselves to others is a hangover-inducing habit that robs us of joy, blinds us to our own gifts, makes gratitude impossible, and feels awful. It is far too easy to slip into a comparison coma — just spend thirty minutes on your Facebook newsfeed, and you may find yourself in one.

Comparison causes us to put unreasonable and unfair expectations on ourselves. Attempting to be like anyone other than yourself is like saying to

God, "I really don't like these particular superpowers you gave me. I want someone else's instead." Conversely, when you get out of envy energy, you can express and share your superpowers while at the same time celebrating the gifts you see in others.

When you feel yourself slipping into a comparison coma, use the Scientist to help you move out of envy and into research. Whatever you see in someone you admire is a positive projection, meaning that they are reflecting back to you something about yourself that you are not fully stepping into or acknowledging. You cannot see in someone else what you do not have inside you. The form in which they express it may be different, but the essence is the same. Comparison gives you clues about what you are truly longing for. Put on your Scientist hat and collect data on the person you envy. Bring that person to mind and complete these sentence stems by writing everything that comes to mind and without overthinking it:

> When I look at you, I see...
> I am jealous of...
> I admire...
> You create...

After you complete your writing, go back and take the other person's name out and turn this positive projection on yourself: replace "you," "yourself," and "your" with "I," "myself," and "my." We can only see in another what we have inside ourselves. You'll realize that the things the other person has or does are also inside you, just expressed in a different way. As you investigate, you will see that what they are expressing or creating is something you are longing for as well. Now it is up to you to do it in your own way. As you stop investing your energy in envy, you will have the capacity to celebrate what you see in them and actually be inspired rather than feeling "less than." Talent, creativity, and success are not limited resources — they are infinite!

EMILY'S STORY

If you work hard, you should expect success, right? But what if success doesn't come fast enough? What if you're burning the candle at both ends and still feel behind others? If only I had such and such like so-and-so has, then life would be perfect. My list went on and on, not only crowding my head and causing me to judge others who had "more," but robbing me of the ability to see the abundance in my life already. I remember waking up each morning, and before I'd even gotten out of bed, I was already spinning in lack. This describes the first thirteen years of my career — it was brutal. And then something happened that was a huge turning point for me when it comes to Expectation Hangovers.

I was hurrying my kids out the door for school. We were running late that day, and I remember yelling at my five-year-old to put on his shoes. Then I yelled at my six-year-old to find his backpack. Then I yelled at both of them to get in the car. And as I slammed the door, jerked the gear into reverse, and turned around to pull out of the driveway, I noticed my oldest son silently crying. His face was red, and his body was clenched tight as he stared at the ground, tears streaming down his cheeks. Good God, what was I doing? In that moment a wave of guilt and shame crashed over me — and I lost it. I buried my face in my hands and had a good old-fashioned, red-eyed, runny-nose, can't-catch-your-breath, u-g-l-y cry.

That was a few years ago — the tipping point of my journey into mindfulness — but I'd been studying enough to know the first step was to get honest about what was really going on. And it had nothing to do with missing backpacks.

It was the fact that I had allowed comparison and my disappointment about where I felt I didn't measure up in my career bleed into every area of my life. Waking up to emails from amazing leaders doing cool stuff was triggering me to go into a dark place that affected how I treated my husband and sons.

And so the next step was to figure out what specifically I was jealous of. What exactly did these people have that I wanted? I sat with that question for months. I carved out a lot of thinking time. I journaled and made lists. And through the process of staying honest, digging deep, and being mindful, I had a tremendous breakthrough.

I thought I was jealous of marquee speaking engagements, bestselling status, and national media coverage. And while that's all well and good, on closer inspection, the quality everyone I analyzed had in common was that they had each created a community around their message. It turns out I wasn't seeking status; I was seeking connection. Once I woke up to the fact that it was my perception — not my circumstances — holding me back, I stopped feeling sorry for myself and started seeking connection in my own way.

Today I'm still not a megabestselling author like the folks I compared myself to, but as I pulled out of the driveway this morning to take my boys to school, I looked at their smiling faces and realized I didn't care anymore where I "should" be. I'm here now — creating a community of my own. And that is what matters most.

"I have an abundance mentality:
When people are genuinely happy at the successes of others, the pie gets larger."
— Stephen Covey

QUICK FIX 5: BE OF SERVICE

"Service to others is the rent you pay for your room here on earth."
— Muhammad Ali

All expectations are created because we want something. Expectations will melt away the instant we switch our mind-set from "What can I get?" to "What can I give?" Adopting a service-oriented mind-set will replace potential Expectation Hangovers with a profound sense of fulfillment.

Serving people is different than pleasing people, which can be selfish. When we serve, we expect nothing. That said, serving is not selfless either because we are not giving to others at the expense of our own needs. Reclaim all the time and energy you have expended on being overresponsible or working to impress others and refocus it on serving others. Trust me, you will have an abundance from which to give, and you will be able to give without attachment or expectation.

"One of the most important lessons of my Expectation Hangover is that being consumed with myself makes it impossible to make an effective and positive impact on others. I want to be able to look back at my life and have peace that I did what I could to help and encourage others."

— Tabitha

To be of service you do not have to drill wells in Africa or volunteer at a homeless shelter. I see so many people not serve because they think they need to do something grandiose. Service is not something you need to schedule in your calendar; it is a way of being rather than a to-do item. Matt serves by being committed to helping people feel they belong, and he will walk up to anyone alone at a party or networking event to make them feel welcome. Jenny serves by using the gift of her sense of humor to make her colleagues laugh in her high-stress investment firm. Jim serves his family by turning off his cell phone each night when he comes home so he is fully present with them. You can serve by opting out of gossiping, by paying people compliments, or by just listening to someone who is sharing with you rather than offering your own viewpoint. And of course, getting involved with a cause or organization is a wonderful way to shift your focus from "me" to "we."

Set the intention each day to serve. Consider asking your Higher Power, "How would you like to use me today?"

People like Mother Teresa, Gandhi, and Martin Luther King Jr., the greatest geniuses of the world when it comes to social change, have made an impact because they worked from a service-oriented mind-set. They laid down their own expectations of life and became channels for a calling. Lay down your own expectations and the "me, myself, and I" mind-set. It's time to open to the loving service mind-set of your beautiful soul.

To cultivate a service consciousness, write a short intention (or call it a prayer if that works for you) that captures how you intend to be of service. It does not have to be long or complex; just attune to your heart and consider how you are drawn to serve. Make this part of your daily ritual by reading or reciting it. What you put your intention toward expands. The more you look toward what you can give, the more you will receive.

QUICK FIX 6: BE A KID

"Joy is the infallible sign of the presence of God."
— Teilhard de Chardin

We take most things, including ourselves, far too seriously! As children, we are naturally playful, creative, and joyful. You didn't have to remember to have fun. You could effortlessly express your emotions. When it came to making a decision, you didn't have to know why or analyze; you chose with your heart. You did not agonize over the past or worry about the future, because you were fully in the present moment. As we grow up, we leave the freedom and beauty of the child behind. But don't fret — he or she is still in there! The child is the embodiment of our most authentic self, freed from judgment, denial, and separation.

Make time for creativity, joy, and play as you did when you were a child. My friend Sam Bennett explains in her book *Get It Done* that we are *all* creative; we just may not all be artistic. Just because you are not drawn to things that are more traditionally thought of as creative, like painting, drawing, or composing music, does not mean you are not creative. Discover what feels creative to you that is an expression of your uniqueness. Creativity is a spiritual practice. It is how the Universe expresses itself through each of us. Yet we often put creativity on the back burner and do not give it the time and attention it deserves!

As you freely play and allow joy, the focus is no longer on who you expect to be or feel you are expected to be, which leaves room for you to explore and be who you *truly* are. You can stop looking for yourself in a therapist's office, foreign country, relationship, or a pair of Jimmy Choos and rediscover yourself in your childlike expression.

And for Pete's sake, find the comedy in your humanness! Laughter is divinely transforming. If an Expectation Hangover knocks at your door, greet it with a sense of humor. Think of the punch lines of great jokes — they tweak our perspective on something so we see it differently. Laugh at the unexpected. Find the humor in how attached you were to your plans when you thought you were the Master of the Universe.

As I write this chapter, it is two weeks before my first draft of the manuscript of this book is due. A few days ago I was racing around town attempting to get errands done because I was leaving town to speak for a week. My day was planned to the minute, and I was serious about getting my to-do list done. Between errand one and two I got in a car accident. Fortunately, no one was hurt. Unfortunately, it was my fault. So not only was I at risk of an Expectation Hangover because things did not go according to my plans, but it was also a perfect setup to be hard on myself for making a mistake.

Although I was not able to avert the accident, I was able to save myself from an Expectation Hangover by not taking the situation seriously. I was responsible and took action in terms of exchanging information with the other driver and reporting the accident to my insurance company. When I got home, I had a good laugh about the situation. How amusing that I had forgotten for a moment that I do not have complete control! And how liberating it felt to be able to have an undesirable situation occur without having to feel the undesirable symptoms of an Expectation Hangover. Granted, not all Expectation Hangovers are laughing matters, but a lot of them can be. Life is serious enough — when you can take yourself more lightly, do so.

QUICK FIX 7: GORGE ON GRATITUDE

"Gratitude is not only the greatest of virtues, but the parent of all others."
— Cicero

If you consume lots of gratitude in your life, you will be too full for disappointment. Being grateful for the pleasant blessings in life is easy, but can you extend appreciation to things that may not be so pleasant, such as your Expectation Hangovers? We become spiritual warriors when we are truly grateful for the circumstances, situations, and people that are challenging. Can you be excited the next time disappointment comes your way and actually grateful for the breakthrough and transformation that await you?

"After my daughter's massive car accident and multiple surgeries, I sold my million-dollar home and downsized to a simple duplex. I learned that life is not a dress rehearsal. Enjoy your friends and family and spend time with those you love while you can. Be happy and content with what you have, always, and don't constantly look for the next thing. Remember that success is not about the money, the house, the car, the trips and travel and diamonds; it is about how you live."

— Denise

Every night before I go to bed, I write a list of things that happened that day and that I am particularly grateful for. Things like a great parking spot, magical moments of serendipity, a fabulous meal, or a laugh with a friend. I also document disappointments, from mini to major, and express my appreciation for growth opportunities. Even if I don't necessarily like what happened, I have gratitude for my ability to choose how to respond to it.

I encourage you to be grateful for all the times you did not get what you wanted or what you expected. Trust me, if things were supposed to go differently, they would have.

Be grateful for all the people who you have felt hurt you. Each has gifted you with an opportunity to forgive and to choose love over blame.

Be grateful for any financial challenges you may be facing and focus on how you are abundant in many other ways. Money does not define you. You are full of earning potential.

Be grateful for the questions in your life and find peace in the unknown. We are not supposed to have it all figured out all the time. Really.

Be grateful for the exact size and shape of your body. Stop making such a big deal over how it looks and start using it to play, create, and move more. I recommend dancing. A lot.

Be grateful for all your losses. Instead of living in the past, feel your grief, and say good-bye to the past and hello to all the wonderfulness that is surrounding you right now.

Be grateful for any health condition you have. See it as a messenger with important and incredibly unique lessons that you get to discover.

Be grateful for all the choices you have made. No more "shoulda, coulda, woulda" thinking. You cannot mess up your destiny. I promise.

Be grateful for all your past, present, and future Expectation Hangovers. Welcome them with open arms, resting in the knowledge that the Surfer, Horseback Rider, Scientist, and Seeker are always there to support and guide you.

"I say thank you for everything. Great food, warm shower, comfy clothes, wonderful smells…everything! When my feet hit the floor in the morning, I say thank you for each foot. I have always been in such a rush in life. My Expectation Hangover taught me to slow down and not only smell the air, but be grateful for each breath."

— Sherri

Be grateful for *everything* and reflect on it daily. I'm sure you've heard the suggestion of keeping a gratitude list. But are you actually doing it? Buy yourself a special gratitude journal and each night write down the things from that day you are grateful for. Be sure not to just include the "good stuff." Use the Horseback Rider to reframe your perception and the Seeker to identify the lessons and blessings. Set the intention to write down at least three things per day, and go from there. Dozing off with appreciation in your heart will positively impact your quality of sleep and the state you wake up in. So get yourself a journal and cuddle up with gratitude.

Go ahead and gorge on gratitude — it's good for you!

> "Stop thinking of gratitude as a by-product of your circumstances
> and start thinking of it as a worldview."
> — Bryan Robles

Put these preventive quick fixes in your pocket and stop engaging in coping strategies that do not work. If you feel an Expectation Hangover coming on, use the Surfer to ride any waves of emotion that may come up, and this time with far more confidence because the waves are no longer unfamiliar and you know that you have safely gotten to the beach before. The Horseback Rider will assist you in whoaing your inner critic and redirecting your beliefs about how your goals are (or are not) taking shape. The Scientist will support you in self-care and help you align your behaviors with what inspires you. The Seeker will help you use everything for your growth and spiritual development, holding your hand when leaps of faith and surrender are required.

CONCLUSION

Creating a life we love from the inside out is not just a possibility; it is our responsibility. It begins by responding to what happens in life in a way that creates ultimate fulfillment and an overflow of love. You are now ready to step out of being a victim of your circumstances and begin creating new ones. You have tools to cure your hangover symptoms and move forward in life in a way that is more aligned with who you truly are rather than relying on expectations as your compass.

The ultimate outcome of overcoming an Expectation Hangover is the experience of *freedom* unconstrained by any external circumstances — a freedom in which you know you have choice in every moment. Fully accepting your spiritual curriculum creates liberation. We begin living in natural harmony and union with the Divine will so that we can not only overcome disappointment, but be grateful for the gifts it brings.

LAUREL'S STORY

In my early twenties I married my best friend and soul mate. We would often look at each other and speak of how lucky we were to have found each other so young. Four and a half years after we married, he died. Becoming a widow at age twenty-seven has been the most intense Expectation Hangover I have experienced. Like any other newlywed, I expected that my twenties would be the most amazing time of my life, and they actually were until the morning of September 3, 1998, when I found out that he had died on a nighttime training mission in his helicopter, along with eleven other men. My entire existence shifted in that moment. All my expectations of marriage, children, traveling together, growing old, having his unconditional love for the rest of my life — all those expectations were shattered. Nothing in my life seemed to make sense without him and us as a reference point. I never even had the chance to say good-bye.

I was devastated, confused, suicidal, depressed, angry, and lonely. I spent most of my time numbing my pain by distracting myself with movies, TV, hanging out with friends, and sleeping — a lot! I withdrew and isolated myself. I stopped working as a nurse for two years and basically moped around trying to pretend that I was handling my life like any other well-adjusted widow. I would often dream of Greg and felt happy and excited when I would see him or talk to him in a dream. In the years of grieving following his death, I drank alcohol as an escape, saw every movie that came to the local theater, and had random sexual encounters. I didn't know consciously at the time what I was doing; I was just doing the best I could to manage the pain and sense of loss of connection. The hardest part was feeling as if I were the only person in the world who was feeling the way I was feeling. I felt like a freakish young widow. I couldn't relate to anyone.

It took me a long time to develop healthy coping strategies that served me in the long term. Walking with my dog was always a very good daily practice. Connecting with nature helped me feel good and kept my body healthy. My mental state was an entirely different issue. I read some books and traveled and talked with friends and family and wrote, but nothing shifted my big issues until I learned tools like reframing and shifting limiting beliefs. I also improved my habits of eating fast food and drinking, by making better choices and implementing several thirty-day processes of abstaining from alcohol, fast food, and casual sex. These coping strategies were about not just external improvement, but also diving deep into my own consciousness and awareness about past hurts, self-defeating talk, low self-esteem, and issues of unworthiness and fear of abandonment. Perhaps the most powerful tool was forgiveness. Forgiving him for dying, forgiving God for taking him from me, and forgiving myself for all the judgments I had made of myself as a young widow.

This process was gradual and time consuming, and involved my complete attention and willingness to change. I worked every level, emotional, mental, physical, and spiritual. Today I am committed to making self-honoring choices and cultivating the most unique and precious relationship I have ever had in my entire life: my relationship with myself. I learned that life is precious and that we live in a world of paradox. That although we are special, unique, and valuable, we are only contributing our small part to the whole. That life is short, but often the day is long. That in knowing myself and trusting myself and being able to rely on myself, I can handle any future event with grace, compassion, and loving awareness. I may not like it, but I have the tools to cope now.

The greatest blessing of my Expectation Hangover is that I now know myself more intimately than I ever could have imagined. I would not have gone on this quest for healing had I not felt broken and in despair. I also have the gift of perspective. Perspective helps me understand how to function at a high level in my day-to-day life and keeps me from honking my horn in LA traffic or being snide to a rude waiter, and in gratitude for the blessings of good health, the ability to go for walks, great food, clean water, and a reliable car. Whenever I feel mired in my own drama or story, I reach out to see who is close by that I can help. How can I be of service? Focusing my energy on using my gifts to help others, and giving freely without concern for what I get in return, is how I prevent Expectation Hangovers. Today, at forty-two, I've never remarried, but I remain open to it and grateful that I had the love that I did share with Greg — even if it did not last forever. Losing the love of my life helped me to rediscover the love that is inside me. It's a beautiful life.

The consciousness of our planet is shifting. People are waking up. You are waking up, and you can thank your Expectation Hangover for the wake-up call. The ability to adapt to new life situations is essential if we are going to successfully respond to the call for change and evolution.

It is the unexpected that truly changes our lives, so stop clinging so hard to your expectations. Open your eyes and heart. Let go of your fear and desire to control. Ditch your plans. Release your expectations. Be ready to be blown away by sensational surprises. And remember that a wonderful gift is always wrapped inside your Expectation Hangover.

ACKNOWLEDGMENTS

I am incredibly blessed to have so many people in my life who have been there for me during my own Expectation Hangovers. To my family, thank you for your unconditional love and support. To all my soul friends, thank you for making me laugh and reminding me who I am when I forget. To all my teachers, thank you for guiding me through the dark times and giving me the tools to navigate my journey with grace. To my spiritual community of USM and MSIA, thank you for being an anchor and holding a container for my growth. To my colleagues and peers, thank you for adding value to this book with your endorsements. To all my clients, readers, story contributors, and workshop participants, thank you for sharing so vulnerably and giving me the opportunity to learn from you as you learn from me.

I'd like to express my deepest gratitude to the many people who have helped make this book possible. To my agent, Michele Martin, thank you for your passion and patience with the process (and me). I could not have done this without your partnership. To Lissa Rankin, for your friendship and for writing such a beautiful and heartfelt foreword. To everyone at New World

Library, I am so proud to be publishing my third book with such a supportive and collaborative group of people. Thank you for joining me on my mission to reframe disappointment. To my personal team of angels who worked with me in putting this book together and took care of me in ways that enabled me to write it: Jill, Angela, Lauren, and Julie.

And to you, the reader, thank you for being willing to step through the transformational doorways that disappointment offers. Your courage to navigate your Expectation Hangovers inspires me.

Finally, I would like to dedicate this book to my very first teacher, Mona Miller, who left this earth way before I was ready for her to go. Mona dedicated her life to helping others live in truth and love. I am eternally grateful, and her profound work lives through me.

Love and Light,
Christine

NOTES

Page 51 *"the application of Loving"*: H. Ronald Hulnick and Mary R. Hulnick, *Loyalty to Your Soul: The Heart of Spiritual Psychology* (Carlsbad, CA: Hay House, 2011), 174.

Page 77 *called self-directed neuroplasticity*: Rick Hanson, *Buddha's Brain: The Practical Neuroscience of Happiness, Love & Wisdom* (Oakland, CA: New Harbinger, 2009).

Page 91 *"We say all the time in teaching"*: "A Conversation with Meditation Teacher and Co-founder of Insight Meditation Society: Sharon Salzberg," *Origin Magazine*, accessed March 24, 2014, www.originmagazine.com /2013/08/04/a-conversation-with-meditation-teacher-and-co-founder -of-insight-meditation-society-sharon-salzberg/.

Page 102 *5 to 10 percent of what most of us do*: Jorn Horstman, behavioral scientist at Dijksterhuis & Van Baaren (D&B).

Page 199 *in her book* Get It Done: Sam Bennett, *Get It Done: From Procrastination to Creative Genius in 15 Minutes a Day* (Novato, CA: New World Library, 2014).

INDEX

acceptance, 30–32, 179, 192–94
accountability, 135
Accountability Partner (exercise),
   138–39
action
   awareness without, 101–2, 140
   compulsive (addictions), 108–9
   during Expectation Hangover,
     104–6
   fear-based, release of, 145
   habits and, 36
   importance of, 140–41
   roadblocks to, 139–40
   value-inspired, 137–38
   See also Scientist Rx (behavioral-
     level treatment plan)
addictions, 108–9
adventure, 135

Agape Love, 145, 152
"aha moments," 101, 169
Alameddine, Rabih, 72
alcohol, 22, 104, 112, 204–5
alcoholism, 156
Ali, Muhammad, 197
American Dream, 146
Angelou, Maya, 86
anger, 46, 62–63, 147, 158–59
Answering Your What-Ifs (exercise),
   94–95
anxiety, 70, 84, 90–91, 116–17
approval seeker (compensatory
   strategy type), 122–23, 128
assumptions, 81
attachment, 185–87
attraction, law of, 71–72
Austen, Jane, 168

authenticity, 65–66, 126–27
avoidance strategies, 21–26, 44, 204
avoidance traps, 131–33
awareness, 27–29, 101–3, 140, 205

Bacon, Francis, 11
balance, 35
Ball, Lucille, 157
beauty, 135
Beckwith, Michael, 117
behavior. *See* action
behavioral-level treatment plan. *See*
    Scientist Rx (behavioral-level
    treatment plan)
Bell, Alexander Graham, 8
Bennett, Sam, 199
blame, 155
body, listening to, 107–8, 111–13
brain
    rewiring, 76–78
    right vs. left, 48
breathing, deep, 91
Brieske, Tim, 44
Brown, Brené, 64
Brown, H. Jackson, Jr., 175
Buddha, 62, 99
Budig, Kathryn, 194
busy bee (compensatory strategy type),
    124

caffeine, 104–5, 107
caretaker (compensatory strategy
    type), 123
Carlson, Richard, 185
Carnegie, Dale, 141
Cayce, Edgar, 150
chameleon (compensatory strategy
    type), 122
changing others, stopping attempts at
    (quick fix 3), 192–94

chaos, 179
childbirth, Expectation Hangovers due
    to, 31–32
children, 50
Christie, Agatha, 3
Cicero, 200
Claiming Your Superpowers (exercise),
    127
Clarifying Your Core Values (exercise),
    134–35
Coelho, Paulo, 178–79
Collecting Data and Formulating Your
    Hypotheses (exercise), 114–15
comedian (compensatory strategy
    type), 123
comfort zones, 15–16, 40, 184
Commitment Contract (exercise),
    138–39
community, 135
comparisons, 128, 194–97
compassion, 51–53, 126–27, 135, 159
    See also self-compassion
Compassionate Self-Forgiveness
    (exercise), 159–61
compensatory strategies
    author's experience, 118–19
    cost of, 121
    development/operation of, 118
    payoffs of, 120–21
    researching (exercise), 125
    superpowers and, 128–29
    types of, 121–24
Connecting to the Present Moment
    (visualization), 92–93
Connecting to Yourself as a Spiritual
    Being (visualization), 150–52
Connecting with Your Own
    Compassion (visualization), 52–53
connection, 135
consciousness, evolving in, 145

contentment, inner, 152–54
contribution, 135
control, 13–15, 31–32, 132
control freak (compensatory strategy type), 122
coping strategies, ineffective, 21–26
Corne, Seane, 67
courage, 99
Cousins, Norman, 159
Covey, Stephen, 197
creativity, 48, 126–27, 128, 131–32, 135, 198–200

dancing, 68
De Bono, Edward, 94
defense mechanisms, 118
depression, 44
diet, 105, 112, 204–5
disappointment
    acceptance and, 29–32
    actions triggered by, 102
    as comfort zone, 16
    creativity and, 48
    as deserved punishment, 17–18, 148
    duration of, and holistic treatment plan, 183–84
    fear and, 8, 132
    leveraging, 5, 40
    pep talks and, 23
    prevention of, 40
    scale of, 11
    as test, 23
    transformation as result of, 12–13
    See also Expectation Hangovers
discipline, 135
Disraeli, Benjamin, 78
distraction, as avoidance strategy, 21–22, 44, 204
Divine, 143
    See also Higher Power

do-overs, 136–37
Downloading Your Purpose (exercise), 174
drug abuse, 22, 44
Dyer, Wayne, 19

eating, 22, 44
electromagnetic field, 145
embarrassment, 46
Emerson, Ralph Waldo, 169
emotional-level treatment plan. See Surfer Rx (emotional-level treatment plan)
emotions
    avoidance/suppression of, 35–36, 41–45, 46–47, 62–63
    creativity and, 48
    during Expectation Hangover, 49–51
    exploring (exercise), 45–46
    expression/release of, 36, 64–67
    fear-based, release of, 145
    making a date with, 67–68
    recycling vs. releasing, 53–56
empathy, 135
energy
    emotional, 68
    motivation and, 135–36
epiphanies, 140
Escaping Your Avoidance Trap (exercise), 132–33
excellence, 135
excitement, 46
exercise (physical), 68, 107, 112, 116–17
exercises
    behavior-level treatment plan, 109–10, 114–15, 125, 127, 132–33, 134–35, 138–39
    emotional-level treatment plan, 45–46, 55–56, 58–59, 60–62, 63

exercises (*continued*)
> Expectation Hangovers, 10–11
> mental-level treatment plan,
>> 72–73, 76, 86–87, 94–95, 97–98
> spiritual-level treatment plan,
>> 159–61, 169–70, 174

Expectation Hangover Assessment
> Form (exercise), 28–29

Expectation Hangovers
> acceptance of, 30–32
> assessment form (exercise), 28–29
> author's experiences, 3–6, 12, 44,
>> 89, 112, 131, 168–69
> avoidance strategies, 21–26, 44
> awareness of, 27–29
> causes of, 11–13
> defined, 8–9
> holistic treatment of, 35–40,
>> 183–84, 189 (*see also* Horseback
>> Rider Rx; quick fixes; Scientist
>> Rx; Seeker Rx; Surfer Rx)
> identifying (exercise), 10–11
> judgments about, 29–30
> symptoms of, 9–10, 49–51, 54,
>> 69–70, 104–6
> transformation as result of, 4–5,
>> 13–19, 179, 203–6
> types of, 9
> untreated, 25

expectations
> age and, 8–9
> fantasy-based, 18–19
> managing, 184–87
> of permanence, 89–90
> values as replacement for, 133–38

expiration dates, 89–90

Exploring Your Emotions (exercise),
> 45–46

Exploring Your Spiritual Curriculum
> (exercise), 169–70

Facebook, 80

"Facilitating Compassionate Self-
> Forgiveness" (university course),
> 160

faith, 37, 135, 178–79

fear
> avoidance traps and, 131–32
> disconnection as result of, 8
> exploring, 46
> future-tripping and, 90
> observation of, 116–17
> release of patterns based in, 145,
>> 206
> self-talk causing, 70
> thoughts grounded in, 75, 84
> what-if questions grounded in,
>> 93–94

financial habits, 105

FINE (Feelings Inside Not Expressed),
> 41

forgiveness
> self-forgiveness, 157–61
> as tool, 155–57, 205

Fox, Michael J., 183

freedom, 135, 203

free falls, 179

friendships, 85–86, 135

Fromm, Erich, 152

fulfillment, sense of, 35, 118, 128–29,
> 131–32, 153, 197

fun, 135

Future Forecasting (exercise), 97–98

future-tripping, 90–92

generosity, 126–27

Get It Done (Bennett), 199

Gibran, Kahlil, 173

goal line, 144–46, 149–50, 172

goals, "secret sauce" for pursuing,
> 185–87

God
    anger at, 63
    belief/disbelief in, 36
    forgiveness of, 205
    as Higher Power, 143
    voice of, 147
    See also Higher Power
Gokey, Danny, 13
gossip, 85–86
gratitude, 200–202, 203
growth, personal, 135
grudge holding, 155
guided visualizations
    for compassion, 52–53
    for internal compass, 38–39
    for the present moment, 92–93
    for spirituality, 150–52
    for surrender, 163–65
guilt, 46, 70, 84, 85–87, 108, 158–59
Gurdjieff, George, 113

habits, 36, 102–3, 105
Hanson, Rick, 76
happiness
    internal nature of, 152–54
    packaging vs., 129–30
Hay, Louise, 111
healing, 51
health
    spiritual growth and, 148–49,
        162–63, 174–75
    worries about, 95–96
high achiever (compensatory strategy
    type), 121–22, 128
Higher Power
    connection with, 35, 36, 152, 203
    disconnection from, 144
    service and, 198
    spirituality and, 143

surrendering oneself to, 161–67
    See also Spirit
Higher Self, 61, 86–87, 149
high involvement–high attachment
    approach, 186
high involvement–low attachment
    approach, 186–87
Horseback Rider Rx (mental-level
    treatment plan)
    exercises, 76, 83–84, 86–87, 94–95,
        97–98
    function of, 74–75
    future-tripping, 90–92
    guided visualizations, 92–93
    past-hacking, 84–87
    tools, 75–76, 78–83
    transformational truths, 89–90
    See also thoughts
Hulnick, H. Ronald, 51
Hulnick, Mary R., 51
humility, 18–19
hypotheses, 103, 113, 114–15

Identifying Your Expectation
    Hangovers (exercise), 10–11
if/then thinking, 16–17
independence, 135
inner contentment, 152–54
insanity, 101
insecurity, 131–32
inside-out living, 152–55, 203
Insight Meditation Society, 91
inspiration, 126–27, 128–29
Instant Whoaing Technique (exercise),
    76
integrity, 135
intention statement, 198
internal compass, connecting to
    (visualization), 38–39
internet, 22

Interpersonal Expectation Hangovers, 9
intimacy, 66, 132
intuition, 37, 126–27, 150, 191–92
involvement, 185–87

Jagger, Mick, 88
Jobs, Steve, 189
John-Roger, 58, 179
journaling, 51, 53, 112, 113–14, 115, 120, 134–35
joy, 128–29, 153–54, 198–200
judger (compensatory strategy type), 124
judgment, 132, 145, 147–48, 155–56, 159, 160–61

Katie, Byron, 27
Keller, Helen, 25
Kenyon, Sherrilyn, 6
King, Martin Luther, Jr., 32
Kleypas, Lisa, 139
Kübler-Ross, Elisabeth, 145

Landers, Ann, 161
Lao-tzu, 137
LaPorte, Danielle, 126
laughter, 199–200
law of attraction, 71–72
leaps of faith, 178–79
learning, 135
Lesser, Elizabeth, 56
lesson quest, 168–71
life purpose, 171–75
life vision, 97–98, 139–40
Lombardi, Vince, 189
Lord, 143
    See also Higher Power
love
    Agape Love, 145
    birth into state of, 7–8, 144

compassion and, 159
as core value, 135
Expectation Hangovers and rediscovery of, 205
judgments and life based in, 147–49
passion as, 173
soul line and, 145
as superpower, 126–27, 128
low involvement–high attachment approach, 186
low involvement–low attachment approach, 185–86
loyalty, 135

Majeski, Paula, 146
Maugham, W. Somerset, 74
meaning, 135
meditation, 91–92, 107, 176
memories, romanticized, 88–90
mental-level treatment plan. See Horseback Rider Rx (mental-level treatment plan)
Miller, Donald, 192
Milne, A. A., 39
mind
    Horseback Rider Rx and, 74–75
    intuition vs., 191–92
    reining in ("whoaing"), 75–76
    reprogramming, 70, 76–78
    See also Horseback Rider Rx (mental-level treatment plan)
mindfulness, 36, 91–92
money, 105
motivation, 135–36
Movement of Spiritual Inner Awareness, 58
Moving into Acceptance (exercise), 30–31

Nature, 143
    See also Higher Power
negativity, 69–70, 78–84, 179
Neill, Michael, 69
neuroplasticity, 77
"next best thing, the," as avoidance
    strategy, 24
numbing techniques, as avoidance
    strategy, 22, 44, 204

observation journal (tool), 113–14, 115
Oneness, 143
    See also Higher Power
other people, acceptance of (quick
    fix 3), 192–94
overexercising, 22, 116–17
overthinking, 101, 125, 195
overwhelmed feeling, 139–40

paralysis by analysis, 101, 125
passion, 172–73
past, romanticization of, 88–90
past-hacking, 84–87
pendulum thinking, 79
people pleaser (compensatory strategy
    type), 122
people pleasing, stopping of (quick
    fix 1), 189–91
pep talks, 23–24
perfectionist (compensatory strategy
    type), 123–24
performance anxiety, 116–17
performer (compensatory strategy
    type), 123
permanence, expectations of, 89–90
playfulness, 126–27, 198–200
prayer, 167, 175–77
present moment, the, 17, 84, 91–93
proactive surrender, 166–67
procrastination, 139–40

quick fixes
    about, 189
    childlike attitude, 198–200
    gratitude, 200–202
    intuition, 191–92
    service, 197–98
    stopping comparisons, 194–97
    stopping people pleasing, 189–91
    stopping trying to change others,
        192–94

recycling, 53–56
redirecting, of thoughts, 78–83
regrets, 70, 84–87, 158, 179
relationships, 109
    See also friendships; romantic
        relationships
release writing (tool/exercise), 56,
    57–59
Releasing Guilt and Regret (exercise),
    86–87
rescuer (compensatory strategy type),
    123
resentment, 155, 158–59
respect, 135
Rewriting Your Story (exercise), 83–84
Roberts, Nora, 101
Robles, Bryan, 202
Rohn, Jim, 41, 109
role-playing Rx's, 39, 183
    See also Horseback Rider Rx
        (mental-level treatment plan);
        Scientist Rx (behavioral-level
        treatment plan); Seeker Rx
        (spiritual-level treatment plan);
        Surfer Rx (emotional-level
        treatment plan)
Rollins, Henry, 49
romanticization, 88–90

romantic relationships
  Expectation Hangovers due to,
    5, 18–19, 36–37, 47, 54–55, 63,
    81–82, 112, 119–20, 136–37,
    157–58, 168–69, 172–73
  past-hacking and, 88
  reinvention in, 90
Rowling, J. K., 21
Russell, Bertrand, 84

sadness, 46, 158–59
Salzberg, Sharon, 91
Satterwhite, Valery, 143
school, Expectation Hangovers due to,
  134
scientific method, 103–4, 113, 114–15
Scientist Rx (behavioral-level treatment
  plan)
  avoidance traps, 131–33
  body awareness, 111–13
  compensatory strategies, 117–25,
    128–29
  exercises, 109–10, 114–15, 125, 127,
    132–33, 134–35, 138–39
  scientist role, 103–4, 113, 126
  self-care plan, 104–10
  superpowers, 126–29, 137–38
  tools, 113–14
  transformational truths, 129–30,
    136–37
  values, 133–38
  See also action
Seeker Rx (spiritual-level treatment
  plan)
  exercises, 159–61, 169–70, 174
  forgiveness, 155–61
  guided visualizations, 150–52,
    163–65
  inside-out living, 152–55, 203
  lesson quest, 168–71

life purpose, 171–75
  spirituality and, 149–50
  surrender to Higher Power, 161–67
  tools, 155–57, 175–77
  transformational truths, 167,
    178–79
  See also spirituality
self, basic, 105–6
self-care plan, 104–10
Self-Care Plan (exercise), 109–10
self-compassion, 52–53, 56, 60, 128,
  159–61
self-expression, 135
self-forgiveness, 157–61
Self-imposed Expectation Hangovers, 9
selfishness, 190–91, 197
self-talk, 70, 78–84, 114, 205
self-trust, 67–68
service, 128, 135, 197–98
sex, casual, 204–5
shame, 46, 65, 158–59
Sinek, Simon, 140
Situational Expectation Hangovers, 9
sleep, 105, 107
social media, 22, 80
soul line, 144–46, 149–50, 172
soul mates, 156–57
Spirit
  connection with, 37, 149
  disappointment as viewed by, 143
  disconnection from, 8
  Expectation Hangovers and
    transformed relationship with,
    150
  fear of judgment by, 17
  forgiveness of, 159
  inside-out living and, 153
  prayers to, 176–77
  surrender to, 162
  See also Higher Power

"spiritual bypass," as avoidance
    strategy, 24–25
spirituality
    basic teachings, 144
    curriculum for, 146–49, 169–70
    defined, 143
    Expectation Hangovers as opening
        to, 143–44, 179, 203–6
    goal line vs. soul line in, 144–46,
        149–50
    inner contentment, 152–54
    Seeker role and, 149–50
    See also Seeker Rx (spiritual-level
        treatment plan)
spiritual-level treatment plan. See
    Seeker Rx (spiritual-level treatment
    plan)
Stewart, Jon, 133
stories, personal, 70–74, 83–84, 98
strength, as avoidance strategy, 23
superhero outfit, 127
superpowers, 126–29, 137–38
suppression techniques, 22
Surfer, the (role-playing Rx), 49–62
Surfer Rx (emotional-level treatment
    plan)
    anger, 62–63
    considerations during, 43–44
    date with emotions, 67–68
    exercises, 45–46, 55–56, 58–59,
        60–62, 63
    guided visualizations, 52–53
    role-playing Rx for, 49–62
    self-care plan, 108–9
    tools, 56, 57–58, 60, 63
    transformational truths, 48, 65–66
    vulnerability and, 64–67
    See also emotions
surrender, 162, 163–67, 179

Surrender as a Spiritual Practice
    (visualization), 163–65

Teilhard de Chardin, Pierre, 198
telephones, 107
television, 22, 44
temper tantrum technique (tool/
    exercise), 56, 60–62, 63
Thoreau, Henry David, 6, 35
thoughts
    control of, 36, 76–78
    exercises, 72–73
    during Expectation Hangover,
        69–70
    fear-based, release of, 145
    law of attraction and, 71–72
    pendulum thinking, 79
    personal stories and, 70–74, 83–84,
        98
    redirecting, 78–83, 98–99
    repetitive, 77
    right/wrong, 148
    See also Horseback Rider Rx
        (mental-level treatment plan)
tolerance, 135
tools
    behavioral-level treatment plan,
        113–14
    emotional-level treatment plan, 56,
        57–58, 60, 63
    mental-level treatment plan,
        75–76, 78–83
    spiritual-level treatment plan,
        155–57, 175–77
transformational truths
    about, 39–40
    authenticity vs. strategy, 65–66
    change, timing of, 167
    creativity as channel, 48
    do-overs, 136–37

transformational truths (*continued*)
  expiration dates, 89–90
  happiness vs. packaging, 129–30
  law of attraction, 71–72
  leaps of faith, 178–79
travel, Expectation Hangovers due to,
  42–43, 154, 177
trust, 135
truth, 135
Twain, Mark, 155
type A (compensatory strategy type),
  122

uncertainty, 131–32
Uncovering Recycled Feelings
  (exercise), 55–56
University of Santa Monica (CA), 160,
  169

validation seeker (compensatory
  strategy type), 122–23, 128
values, 133–38
vulnerability, 23, 64–67, 132

Walsch, Neale Donald, 147
what-ifs, 94–97
when/then thinking, 16–17
whoaing (tool/exercise), 75–76

widowhood, Expectation Hangover
  due to, 204–5
Wiersbe, Warren Wendel, 53
Williamson, Marianne, 68, 144
Winfrey, Oprah, 131
wisdom, 126–27, 135
work
  Expectation Hangovers due to,
    3–4, 12, 14–15, 18, 50–51, 59–60,
    74, 80–81, 82–83, 93–94, 106,
    107–8, 111–12, 119–20, 165, 169,
    170–71, 187, 195–97
  as numbing technique, 22, 44
  past-hacking and, 88
  reinvention in, 90
workaholism, 114, 128
worry, 70, 84, 94–97
Wright, Judith, 54
writing
  comparisons, 195
  intention statement, 198
  life vision, 97–98
  release writing, 56, 57–59
  See also journaling

yoga, 112
Your Storyboard (exercise), 72–73

ABOUT THE AUTHOR

Christine Hassler left her job as a successful Hollywood agent to pursue a life she could be passionate about. In 2005, she wrote a guidebook for quarter-life women, *20 Something, 20 Everything*. Her second book, *The 20 Something Manifesto*, written for men and women, stemmed from her experience as an expert on the quarter-life crisis.

As a life coach, Christine supports individuals of all ages in discovering the answers to the questions "Who am I?" "What do I want?" and "How do I get it?" She is also a speaker and leads seminars and workshops around the world at colleges, personal growth events, conferences, and corporations. Christine has appeared as an expert on the *Today* show, CNN, ABC, CBS, FOX, E!, Style, and PBS, as well as various local television and radio shows. She is also a frequent contributor to the *Huffington Post*, the Daily Love, and *Cosmo*. She frequently hosts transformational retreats in beautiful and magical destinations such as Costa Rica, Bali, Laguna Beach, Australia, and Tulum, Mexico.

Christine is a member of Northwestern University's Council of 100 and the Young Entrepreneur Council and is on the faculty of the University of Santa Monica, where she teaches spiritual psychology.

Christine graduated cum laude from Northwestern University and received her master's degree in Spiritual Psychology with an emphasis on Consciousness, Health and Healing from the University of Santa Monica. She is active in volunteerism and loves living a healthy lifestyle — which means lots of green juice, yoga, hiking, and laughing! She currently resides in Los Angeles and loves spending time with her family and friends in Austin, Texas. Her website is www.christinehassler.com.

ADDITIONAL SUPPORT ON YOUR JOURNEY THROUGH EXPECTATION HANGOVERS

Join Christine's community by signing up for her FREE weekly blog and vlog for a regular dose of radical self-reflection with practical direction:
www.christinehassler.com

Download a FREE copy of Christine's ebook,
32 Days to Uplevel Your Mind and Uplift Your Heart:
www.christinehassler.com/sign-up-for-your-free-gift

Grab your copy of her guided meditation CD, *Meditation Rx:*
Guided Meditations to Treat Your Mind and Heart:
www.christinehassler.com/meditation-cd

Sign up for one of her online courses here:
www.christinehassler.com/books-and-courses

JOIN CHRISTINE LIVE AT A RETREAT OR WORKSHOP

Christine hosts three- to five-day retreats around the world.
Go here to learn more:
www.christinehassler.com/events-workshops

GET COACHED BY CHRISTINE

Christine partners with four clients a year for six-month
one-on-one transformational programs. Learn more here:
www.christinehassler.com/coaching-christine

Join the "Secret Sauce" Mastermind Group and learn how to leverage
your unique gifts and experiences to live your purpose.
For more information, email jill@christinehassler.com.

ENGAGE WITH CHRISTINE ONLINE

Like her on Facebook and post your "aha's" and questions:
www.tinyurl.com/christinehassler

Connect with her on Twitter:
@christinhassler (use hashtag #expectationhangover)

Follow her on Instagram:
www.instagram.com/christinehassler
(use hashtag #expectationhangover)

Follow her on Pinterest:
www.pinterest.com/chassler2

Subscribe to her YouTube channel:
www.youtube.com/user/christinehassler